PIRACY ON THE GREAT LAKES

TRUE TALES OF FRESHWATER PIRATES

MIKEL B. CLASSEN

Additional Illustrations
by Joanna Walitalo and Bruce Denomie

Modern History Press

Ann Arbor, MI

Piracy on the Great Lakes: True Tales of Freshwater Pirates
Copyright © 2025, 2026 by Mikel B. Classen
All Rights Reserved.
Additional illustrations by Joanna Walitalo and Bruce Denomie

ISBN 979-8-89656-003-6 paperback
ISBN 979-8-89656-004-3 hardcover
ISBN 979-8-89656-005-0 eBook

Published by
Modern History Press   www.ModernHistoryPress.com
5145 Pontiac Trail   info@ModernHistoryPress.com
Ann Arbor, MI 48105

Tollfree 888-761-6268   FAX 734-663-6861

Distributed by Ingram Book Group: USA, CAN, EU, AU

Audiobook available from Audible and iTunes

Library of Congress Cataloging-in-Publication Data

Names: Classen, Mikel B., author.
Title: Piracy on the Great Lakes : true tales of freshwater pirates / Mikel
  B. Classen.
Description: Ann Arbor, MI : Modern History Press, 2025. | Includes
  bibliographical references and index. | Summary: "A survey of documented
  pirates across the Great Lakes basin including Dan Seavey, Jesse James
  Strang, William (Bully) Henry Hayes. From the days of French-Canadian
  voyageurs through the post-Civil War period, an account of cargoes,
  crews, and ships is included. Special focus on enforcement by the USS
  Michigan"-- Provided by publisher.
Identifiers: LCCN 2024062190 (print) | LCCN 2024062191 (ebook) | ISBN
  9798896560036 (paperback) | ISBN 9798896560043 (hardback) | ISBN
  9798896560050 (epub)
Subjects: LCSH: Piracy--Great Lakes Region (North America)--History. |
  Pirates--Great Lakes Region (North America)--History. | Michigan (Paddle
  steamer)--History. | Great Lakes Region (North America)--History.
Classification: LCC F551 .C53 2025 (print) | LCC F551 (ebook) | DDC
  910.4/5--dc23/eng/20250203
LC record available at https://lccn.loc.gov/2024062190
LC ebook record available at https://lccn.loc.gov/2024062191

Contents

Table of Figures

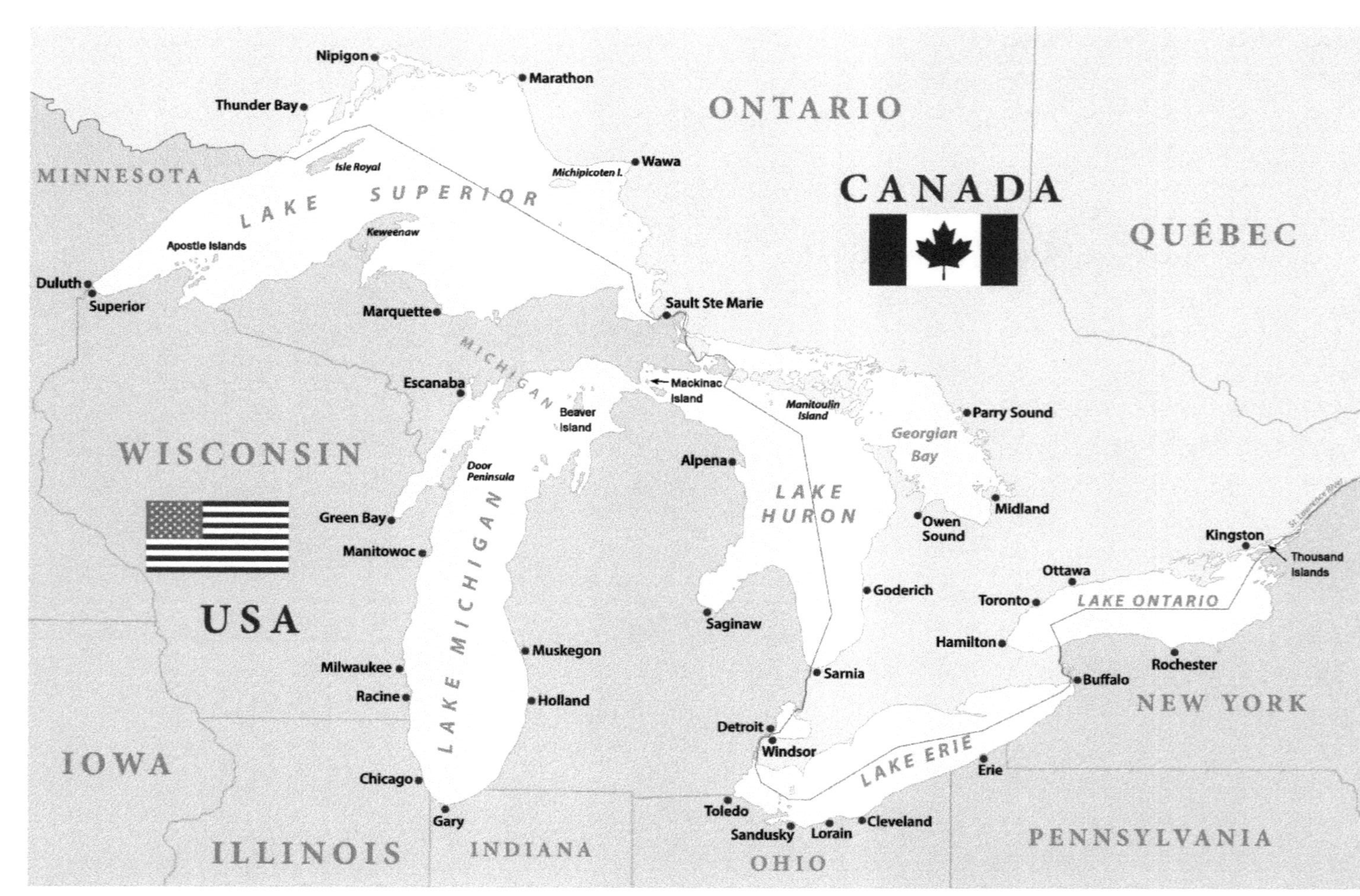

Nipigon
Marathon
Thunder Bay
ONTARIO
Wawa
Michipicoten I.
MINNESOTA
Isle Royal
LAKE SUPERIOR
CANADA
QUÉBEC
Apostle Islands
Keweenaw
Duluth
Superior
Marquette
MICHIGAN
Sault Ste Marie
Escanaba
Mackinac Island
Manitoulin Island
Parry Sound
Beaver Island
Georgian Bay
WISCONSIN
Door Peninsula
Alpena
LAKE HURON
Midland
Owen Sound
Green Bay
USA
Manitowoc
Goderich
Kingston
Thousand Islands
Ottawa
Toronto
LAKE ONTARIO
Saginaw
Hamilton
Muskegon
Milwaukee
Rochester
Racine
Holland
Buffalo
Sarnia
NEW YORK
Detroit
Windsor
IOWA
LAKE ERIE
Erie
Chicago
Toledo
Gary
Sandusky
Lorain
Cleveland
ILLINOIS
INDIANA
OHIO
PENNSYLVANIA
LAKE MICHIGAN

1 Pirates and Piracy on the Great Lakes

Piracy has always been with us. On the Great Lakes, piracy was different than depicted in Hollywood's glorified *Pirates of the Caribbean*. No Aztec gold was heading back to Spain on armadas. But there were pirates just the same.

Instead of chasing down ships laden with gold, the Great Lakes pirates were after commodities. There were fur pirates, timber pirates, religious pirates, and inept pirates. Just about anything that could be sold fell prey to pirates. Though there was no Spanish gold, there was loot to be had. Payrolls were shipped and moneys for banks and treasuries were consigned. Cargos could be stolen and then sold at the next port.

And, there was much to be had. Commerce on the Great Lakes grew at a blinding rate. Merchants were building ships eventually filling the waters with traffic. There were no roads or railroads yet, the Great Lakes were the highways of their day. Over 300 ships were launched in one year on Lake Erie alone. This presented endless opportunities for piracy and naturally many accepted the calling. Piracy thrived on the Great Lakes.

For our purposes, piracy is defined as attacking, robbing, and hijacking on the water. From Lake Superior to Lake Erie, piracy cropped up throughout history. This would be a much larger book if it were not for the nature of piracy. Secrecy and stealth coupled with leaving no witnesses casts much of the acts of piracy in darkness. No witnesses are the best witnesses. Many incidents we simply don't know about. But we do know pirates were out there.

Waiting in the night, hidden behind a remote island, no lights showing, pirates would lure unsuspecting ships into unknown waters. Then they would silently slide up to them and board the ship. The crew would be killed and the bodies thrown over the side, weighted down with chains. The pirates would take the cargo, sink or burn the ship, and then just as quietly, sail away into the night. Dead men tell no tales, nor do they testify in court.

Ships and crews disappeared into oblivion on the Great Lakes. Much of it was attributed to storms, but pirates also roamed these waters, and many ships were lost due to pirate raids. These pirates weren't the swashbucklers of film, but men who used guns and knives and were brawlers and drinkers, roaming the fresh waters of a lawless frontier. Of course, many of these incidents and stories will be forever lost to time. In this book, I will present as many as I could verify as documented. Some of them even include first-person reports to put you right in the picture. Still, this book can only skim the surface of a much larger world of piracy that was practiced throughout the Great Lakes.

The only law on the Great Lakes in the nineteenth century was a ship known as the *USS Michigan*. Launched in 1844, it was the only gunship within the Great Lakes. Early on, it would patrol Lakes Erie, Huron, and Michigan. After the Soo Locks were built in 1855, Lake Superior would be added to its patrol area.

The *Michigan* was the first ironclad ship built by the young US government to patrol the lakes and the border with Canada. Its mandate was to prevent piracy and rebellion. It plays a large role in several of the piracy stories. The ship was retired in 1912 under the name of *Wolverine*. For nearly seven decades, the *Michigan* plied the waters of the Lakes, doing its best to enforce the laws of the federal government.

As you can imagine, patrolling the Great Lakes in those early years was a massive job. A single ship, however formidable, was inadequate for the task. While the *Michigan* was on one lake, the other lakes were open to exploitation. The opportunity was too big not to take advantage of. The Great Lakes were ripe, and pirates were there to do the picking.

USS Michigan refitted as the training ship USS Wolverine

Crew of USS Wolverine drills at Erie dock

2   Piracy of the Fur Trade

In the 1700s and early 1800s, fur was gold. The demand for it was voracious. Beaver was the popular fur of the time used for hats and coats. The Great Lakes frontier was full of furs, and Lake Superior, northern Minnesota, and into the Canadian frontier were prime sources for the furs. In the early years, the French claimed much of the region for "New France," and the French explorers and voyageurs would create a water trail known as the Voyageur's Highway. This route ran from Montreal, Canada, deep into the heart of north central Canada, through Lake Winnipeg to Lake Athabasca.

Canoes could carry up to two tons of furs. The canoes were thirty-five feet long and usually had six men paddling, but some canoes could get up to sixty-five feet long with a dozen men paddling. The small canoes could haul up to two tons of furs and the larger canoes at least double that.

Fur values varied by season and the current whims of fashion. For a long time in the 1800s, a beaver hat was the mark of a distinguished gentleman, and everyone wanted one. A finished hat could be had for about $30 prior to 1850, and this drove the prices trappers earned for pelts. In general, beaver and otter were the most desirable pelts, and in the 1870s and 1880s, they would go for about $6 US dollars a pelt. Pelts were sold by the pound, at about $4 a pound, and a full pelt usually averaged 1.5 pounds; hence, the $6 a pelt figure. Most other animal pelts, such as raccoon, were valued much less.

The Voyageur's Highway
Hudson Bay
Fort Chipewyan
Lake Athabasca
Fort McMurray
James Bay
Norway House
Lake Winnipeg
Cumberland House
Fort Albany
Winnipeg River
Lake Superior
French River
Montreal
Ottawa River
Lake Huron
Lake Michigan
Lake Ontario
Lake Erie
0   200   400Km
Voyageur's Highway
Montreal to Fort Chipwyan

Typical fur trade fort (engraving)

Trading for furs (engraving)

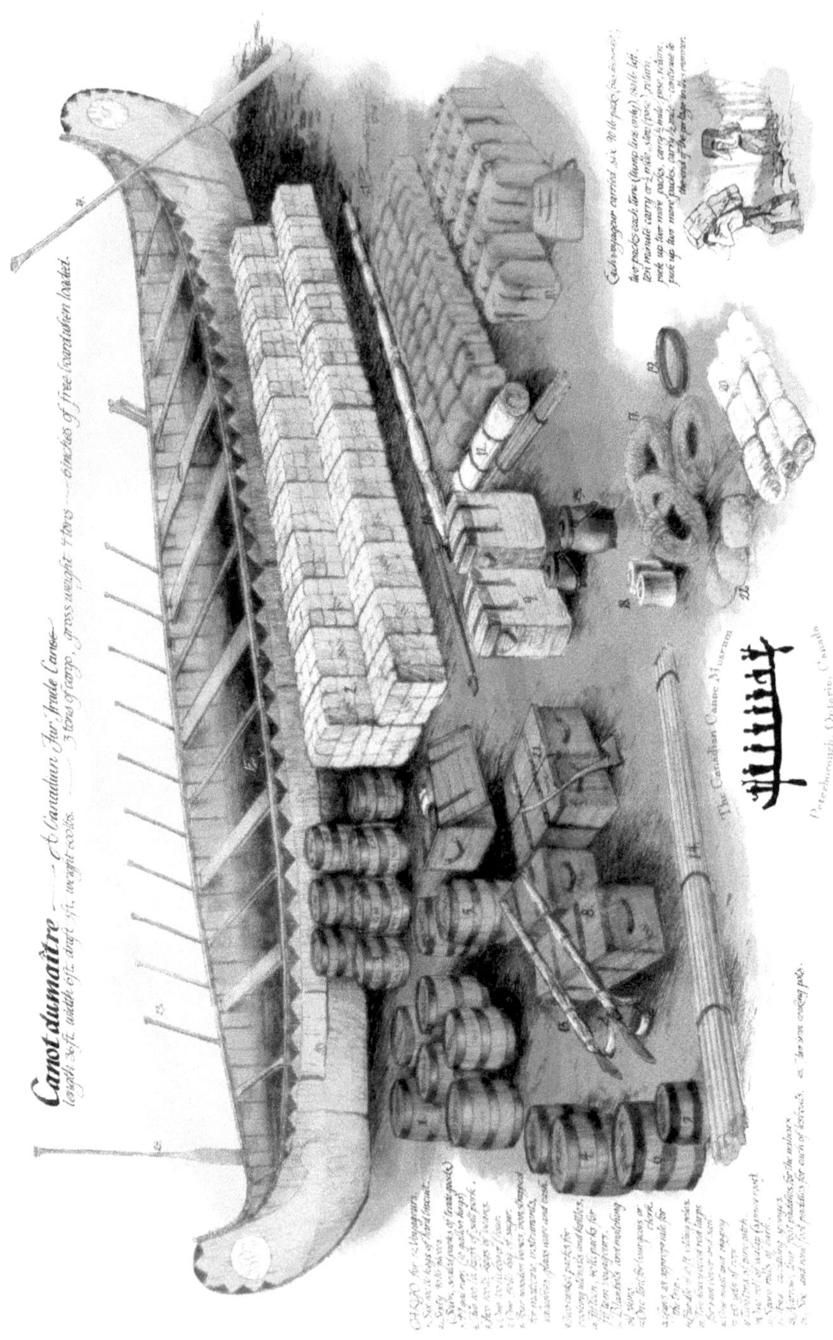

Canots du maître– the "Master Canoes"

Let's return to our canoe with a two-ton load of pelts. Such a vessel would be laden with at least 2,500 of these 1.5-pound pelts, with a street-value of $15,000 in 1850 (again using $6 per pelt for beaver). Taking into account inflation, that same canoe load would be worth more than $350,000 in 2025 purchasing power. Often, individual pelts weren't sold for cash at all—they were traded by barter to obtain something else of value, including food, cloth, rifles, and ammunition. For these kinds of transactions, no written price averages existed; each trading post did its own valuation, and the owners kept their price schedules in their heads.

While the French were claiming New France, The British had set up shop further north in Hudson and James Bay. This was the founding of the Hudson Bay Company. They were immediate rivals with the French and applied every ruthless tactic a cutthroat business could provide. They condoned theft, murder, and piracy against rival trappers.

Rival trappers and companies would attack the voyageur canoes, kill the occupants, and run off with their cargo. When the French gave up Canada to the British, the French voyageurs now had to work for someone they completely despised and someone who despised them back. The Hudson's Bay Company, which had been operating in the far north, now moved to take over the void left by the exit of the French.

A new British company set up shop in the New World. The Northwest Fur Company moved into the Great Lakes. Two British fur companies, the Hudson's Bay Company and the Northwest Fur Company, worked the Lake Superior shoreline. Hudson's Bay Company operated on the north side and the Northwest on the south side. These two companies went to war with each other. They would attack one another's canoes, steal their cargo, and kill the occupants. These raids were constant. The war even led to a massacre in the Red River Country north of Minnesota.

The voyageurs' canoes were on constant lookout for attacks either by the Native tribes—the Natives could steal the furs and sell them to the other guy too—or other trappers with a mind to cash in on another man's labors. When the only law in the wilderness was the companies, murder was easy to get away with. Both companies built fur trade forts that were established along various routes to collect and transport the furs as well as protect themselves from the fur pirates.

One story from Lake Superior is about the Apostle Island Pirates. The Apostle Islands are a group of spectacular islands near Bayfield, Wisconsin. It is a rugged region with jagged rock formations creating a dangerous area to sail ships in. It was also an excellent hideaway. An article printed in the *Bayfield County Press* is the only source for this story, and it was written several years after it happened. It reads:

> There once was a band of adventurous pirates known as the "Apostles," and their chief. In the latter part of the eighteenth century they made their rendezvous among the outer Apostle Islands and Oak Island in particular, where they were protected from sudden attacks by the rugged shores. For a time the pirates met with wonderful success. They not only robbed traders and voyageurs, but they plundered a party of French capitalists who were on their way to the newly discovered copper mines at French River on the north shore. The pirates killed the entire party except the mining engineer, from whom they expected to gain a knowledge of the proposed mining operations. The pirates made a real warship out of the little vessel of the murdered capitalists and this eventually proved the means of the discovery and capture of the pirates. The whereabouts of the war vessel was learned and an expedition sent against it took the pirates by surprise. The apostles, Mathew, Mark, Luke and John, with Judas the first lieutenant, and Phillip, the secretary, along with the Chief and the other six, were taken to Montreal where all but the Chief were executed. The Chief was related to the commanding officer and simply disappears from history.

Unfortunately, no more details have come to light about these pirates, but the story has been held up by some as the source for how the Apostle Islands got their name. There is a tale that the pirates left behind, on Oak Island, a treasure of French gold that was taken from the capitalists in the raid. No treasure has ever been found, but it remains as a legend of Lake Superior.

Fur trade piracy was such a nuisance that forts were built along the shore of the lakes to collect the furs. The Northwest Fur Company built sailing ships to sail a route on Lake Superior from fort to fort collecting the furs and then carry the entire load to the Sault. Eventually, the Northwest Fur Company went bankrupt and all of its holdings went to the Hudson's Bay Company. This ended the war between companies, so the fur trade routes quieted down.

As the region changed hands, first the French, then the British, and eventually the Americans would enter the scene. The British had lost the colonies, and when Thomas Jefferson made the Louisiana Purchase in 1803, much of the Great Lakes became American territory. In 1824, John Jacob Astor was given all the rights to the American fur trade and immediately began fur trading on the southern shores of the Great Lakes and all of Lake Michigan. Now an attack by or against the British in Canada would mean an international incident and a trade war would mean a real war. However, a few years later, the popularity of fur died off so it lost its profitability.

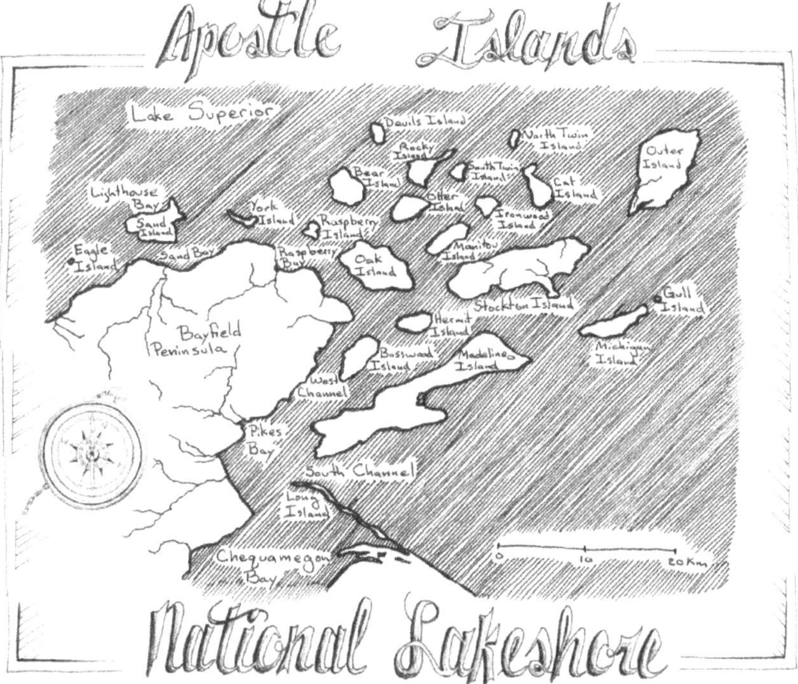

3 William Johnson: Pirate or Privateer?

William Johnson was dubbed "The Pirate of the St. Lawrence." He sailed in the St. Lawrence River near the Thousand Islands off the coast of New York. Johnson and his crew robbed and looted up and down the St. Lawrence River.

Johnson was born in Quebec in 1782 and grew up in Bath and Kingston in Upper Canada. He opened a store with his brother as a partner. They did well enough that they owned their own sailing ship for trade. In 1812, as the war broke out, Johnson found himself being accused as a smuggler and made claims that he had deserted the militia. There were rumors he had spied for the Americans. William Johnson lost everything and was forced to flee to the United States. This naturally caused a strong dislike for the British and he vowed vengeance on what he had considered abuse.

He landed in Sackett's Harbor with his family and then moved on to French Creek (today Clayton). It was here that he found several men that sympathized with his plight and joined up with him. They began a private war against the Canadian British. Johnson and his crew soon occupied several islands. Grindstone, Powder, Abel's, and Wells also known as Wellesly which was their main hideout. The hideout was described as "a series of underground passages and apartments partly excavated and partly natural caves, secure under any attack, much like the cavern home of the refugees in Jules Verne's *Mysterious Island*."

It was from this place that Johnson's pirates set out with boats of six oars, small and swift. They were quieter than sailing ships and they could slip alongside of their victims unseen and unheard in the night. The small boats thought swift when under power of the oars, they were equipped with sails for fast getaways too. They would strike quick and silent harassing the British crippling many of their supply ships.

Johnson himself was said to look like a true Buccaneer. He carried "six pistols, a dirk, a Bowie knife in his belt and a sword." He was "tall, well built, swarthy, ruddy complexioned, keen-eyed, and was an able fearless fighter. It was said he was worth fifty men in a fight." His ship and crew roamed the Islands, smuggling and waylaying rich British cargo ships.

Johnson's daughter grew up and became a member of his crew. Kate was known as "the Queen of the Thousand Islands." She would work as Johnson's spy. Using her good looks and wealthy mannerisms, she could work her way into the confidence of many. She would often bring supplies to Johnson's hideout in the Islands, able to navigate them with ease, she was a lifeline for the pirates.

Then in 1837, the Canadian Revolution broke out. Yes, Canada actually revolted against British rule. They called it the Patriot War. Johnson met up with two Canadian revolutionaries, William Lyon Mackenzie, and self-appointed "General" Van Rensselaer, at their "Patriot" camp on Navy Island in the Niagara River. While they were there, Canadian raiders, captured an American steamship named *Caroline*. They burned it and sent it over Niagara Falls. Johnson was said to have shouted "I'll get even with you damn Tories yet!"

Johnson and Van Rensselaer returned to the St. Lawrence area where there were many anti Canadian sympathizers. Van Rensselaer appointed Johnson as the revolutionary "Admiral of the Eastern Navy." Johnson was given the duty of organizing men for their "war."

Once again, Johnson used the pretense of war and chaos to loot British ships. He attacked the steamer *Sir Robert Peel* near Wells Island. The steamer needed fuel and had pulled into the island to take on fuel. Dressed as Indians, he and his crew looted everything on the ship and then made the passengers give up their money and valuables. It was estimated that the pirates stole £15,000 in personal

The Pirate William Johnson (engraving)

items and also got £20,000 in gold bullion from a payroll bound for Canadian soldiers.

They loaded the passengers onto his ship, emptied the holds of the cargo. They then deposited the passengers on shore and torched the *Sir Robert Peel*. She burned to the waterline. Johnson reportedly told the Captain of the *Peel*, "We wouldn't have burned your ship, only to get even with your friends who burnt our *Caroline* at Niagara." Then Johnson sailed away. The result of this attack was a price on Johnson's head.

The Governor General of Canada, the Earl of Durham, issued a £1,000 reward for the capture of Johnson and any of his crew. The

Governor of New York also posted a reward of $500 and $100 apiece for apprehension of any of the crew.

One daring move of Johnson's was to smuggle in American sympathizers across the border into Canada. Johnson was doing just that when he was caught on the New York side of the border—there was an attempt to prosecute him for piracy over the burning of the *Sir Robert Peel*. Johnson claimed that he was Commander in Chief of the Patriot Naval Forces and was working for the great cause for independence of Canada. He was a Canadian citizen, and he wasn't able to be tried. He even produced a slip of paper stating he was Commander in Chief, but the signature on the paper was his own. The paper read:

> I, William Johnson, a natural born citizen of Upper Canada, certify that I hold a commission as commander-in-chief of the naval forces and flotilla. I commanded the expedition that captured the steamer *Sir Robert Peel*. The men under my command in that expedition were nearly all natural born English subjects—the exceptions were volunteers for the expedition. My headquarters was on an island in the St. Lawrence, without the jurisdiction of the United States, at a place named by me, Fort Wallace. I am well acquainted with the boundary line, and know which of the islands belong to the United States; and in the selection of the island I wish to be positive and not locate within the jurisdiction of the United States, and had reference to the decision of the commissioners under the 6th article of the Treaty of Ghent, done at Utica, in the state of New York, 13th June, 1822. I know the number of the island, and by that decision it was British territory. I yet hold possession of that station, and we also occupy a station some twenty or more miles from the boundary line of the United States, in what was his majesty's dominions until it was occupied by us. I act under orders. The object of my movement is the independence of the Canadas. I am not at war with the commerce or property of the citizens of the United States.

Signed this tenth day of June, in the year of our Lord one thousand eight hundred and thirty eight.

[signed] WILLIAM JOHNSON

Though the document was an obvious forgery, the Americans decided to let him go with a warning to stay out of Canadian affairs. They refused to indict him. If he would have been caught on the Canadian side, the outcome would likely have been different. Canada was actively hanging the revolutionary "Patriots" whenever they were caught including one of Johnson's men that was a part of the burning of the *Sir Robert Peel*. There was little doubt of his fate if the Canadians caught him.

Eventually, the revolution died out, but Johnson continued to raid, loot, and burn the shipping, in particularly Canadian shipping, around the Thousand Islands area. He still had it out for the British. A hunt for Johnson was mounted by both sides. The Thousand Islands were hard to search—the islands were thick with forests and swamps. They had served Johnson well as a hideout. He took refuge

**Contemporary re-imagining of a woodcut
"The Burning of the *Sir Robert Peel*" (1838) by F. C. Curry**

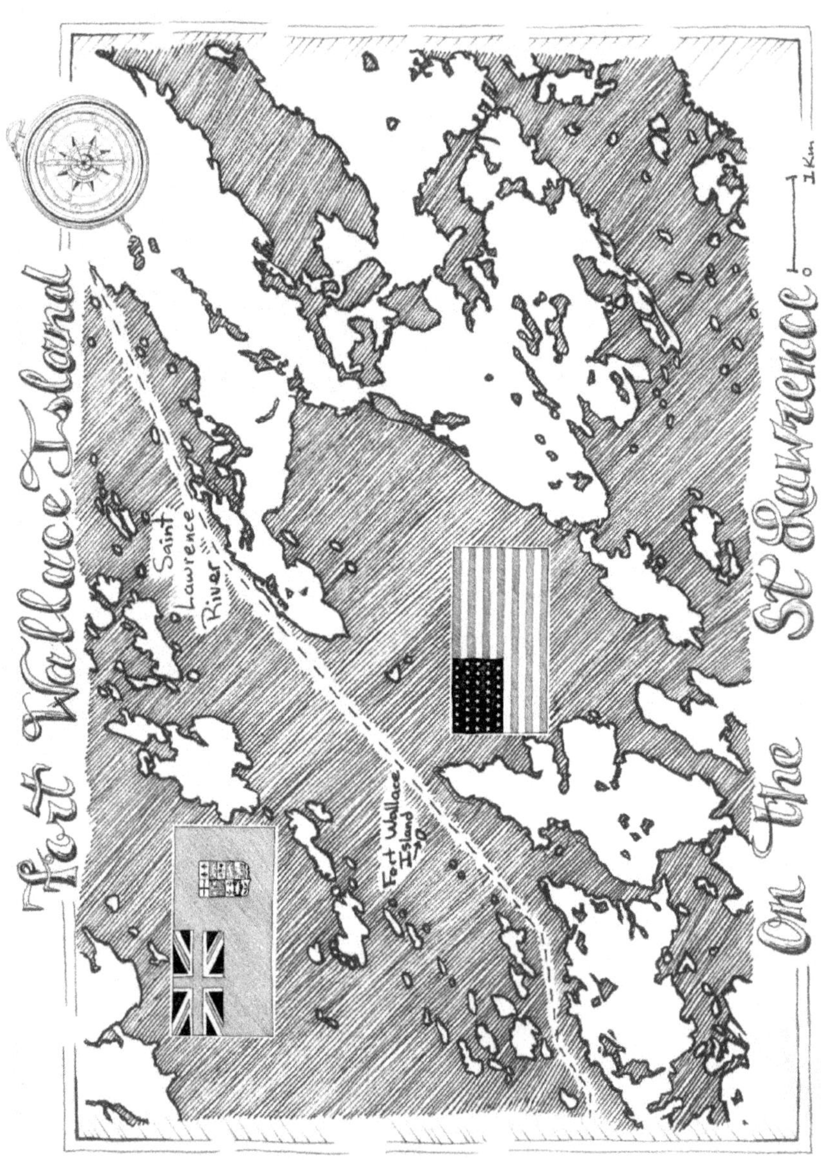

Ft. Wallace Island on the St. Lawrence

in a place called Devil's Oven. It was a cave that had an invisible opening that acted like an oven door. Their raids were done with longboats so when they were pursued, they could portage across the islands and hide in the thickets where no one could follow.

Kate, Johnson's daughter, would often run supplies to them as it seemed she was the only one able to pass unquestioned. Her knowledge of the islands was only surpassed by her father. There were stories told of her prowess at paddling a canoe alone, through the islands day or night to bring her father and his men food and news of the hunt for them.

Johnson tried to participate in a last engagement called the Battle of the Windmill, with his group of Patriots to attack a small village near Kingston. The battle went badly as several of the attacking ships including Johnson's became stuck on a large sandbar. Johnson was able to free a couple of the ships but it was too little too late. They lost the battle and the revolution died as most of the leaders were captured and put on trial in Kingston where they were eventually hanged. Johnson got away.

Out of frustration, the Americans joined the British searching for Johnson. The situation didn't improve. When his hideout was finally located on Able Island, or as another source says at Wells Island, an attempt was made to arrest Johnson and his crew. All escaped but two, and Johnson was one of the escapees. The only thing the searchers got for their troubles was Johnson's twelve-oared rowboat.

Eventually "Pirate Bill" would be caught by the Americans and was placed in custody at the Ogdensburg jail. He quickly escaped. A manhunt ensued and he was recaptured and brought to Albany for trial. He was found guilty of breach of neutrality laws and sentenced to one year in jail and $200 fine. In an amazing act of loyalty, Kate voluntarily shared her father's imprisonment!

Most of the people of Albany were sympathetic towards the prisoners as many supported the Patriot revolution to throw off the yoke of Britain and felt Johnson was wrongly jailed. William and Kate became "the most noted prisoners of the age." Many people made it a point to visit them such as statesmen and the area elite.

After seven months, Johnson and his daughter Kate escaped. A group of friends had gotten together and broke them out.

Pirate Bill went back to the Thousand Islands. He warned anyone that he would kill them if they bothered him. Kate had had her fill. She loved her father deeply, but she knew he was on a road to his demise. She was determined to not allow that to happen. She got up a petition and asked for a pardon for her father. There were thousands of signatures on it.

A Presidential pardon, signed by President Harrison in 1840, came his way absolving him of his past crimes. He was given the post of lightkeeper for the Rock Island Lighthouse, not far from where he had burned the steamer *Sir Robert Peel*.

In later years he would act as a fisherman and guide living a quiet and idyllic life. He died in his bed in 1870 at 83 years old. His daughter Kate had a pleasant later life. She married and had several children. She had kept a gold chain taken from one of the passengers of the *Sir Robert Peel* and had it divided into four and gave it as an heirloom to her four daughters. Her fame as the Queen of the Thousand Isles inspired poems, articles and even a play was written about her and staged in New York.

4 James Jesse Strang, the Pirate King

The moonless night made the blackened sails difficult to spot from the shore. Men lined the gunwales of schooners and fishing boats as they approached the tiny village. Silently, the ships slipped into the small harbor of St. Helena Island. The anxious men crawled over the sides and made their way to town. Surprise was always their advantage. They looted and pillaged everything they could carry. The sleeping villagers had no time to react. The pirates looted their food stores and carried off much of the livestock. They took fishing boats and nets along with the preserved catches. Anything that wasn't tied down, they took. By the time the townspeople could react, the raiders were on their way back to their ships. Any who resisted the looting would be beaten or killed. Much of their food and stores were now gone. If they couldn't get more, starvation would be a very real possibility. Even if they could get more, would the pirates just come back and do it again?

That was a very real possibility with the Mormon pirates raiding the islands of the Straits of Mackinac. They would come in the night and sail away as quickly as they had come. The self-proclaimed king of the Mormon settlement, James Jesse Strang, had declared that God had told him that the islands of the Straits were for the Mormons and it was their land for the taking. Anyone else was trespassing, and the Mormons saw it as their right to take anything from those islands as theirs.

Strang's story begins in 1844 when the budding religion of Mormonism was on the rise. Joseph Smith, the founder of the religion, had established an elders council of twelve. On it was

The Pirate James Jesse Strang

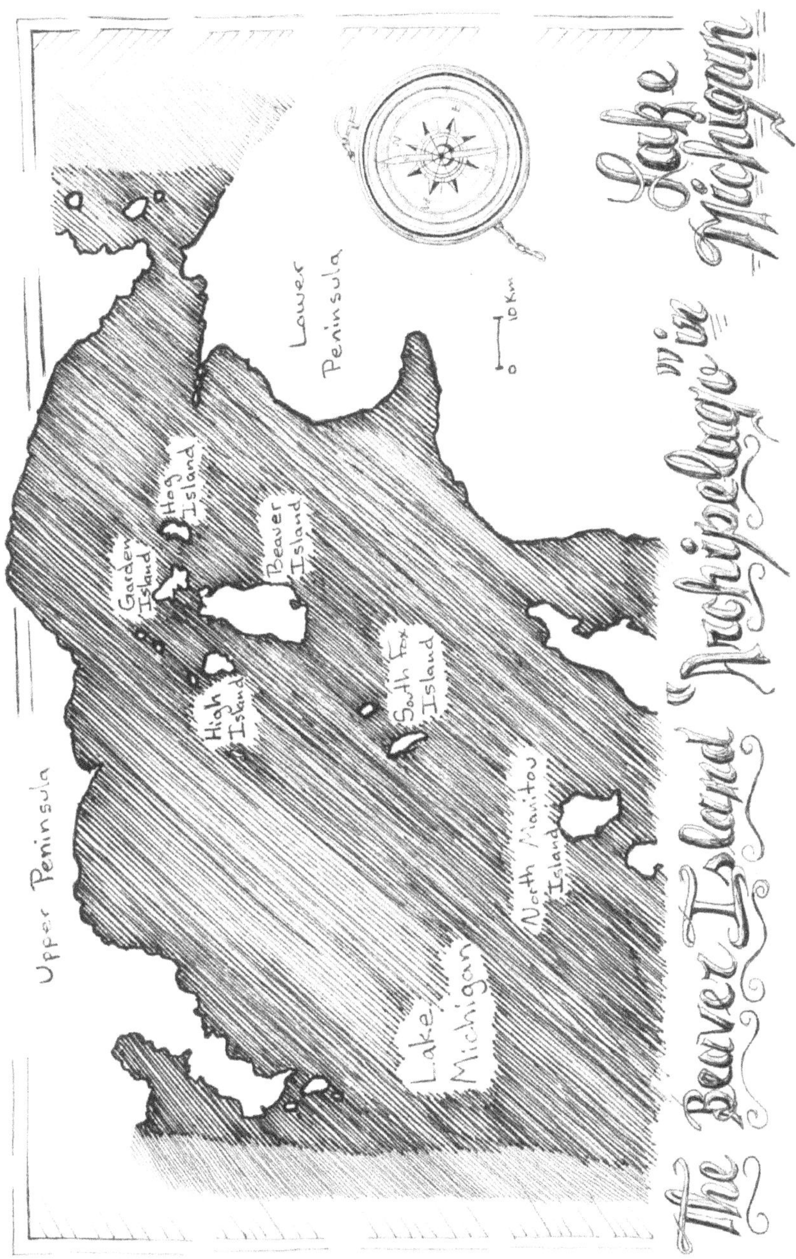

The Beaver Island Archipelago in Lake Michigan

Brigham Young and an upcoming Mormon leader named James Jesse Strang. He was a brilliant and conniving individual with visions of grandeur. Strang had managed a meteoric rise within the inner Mormon circle.

The Mormons believed that an angel had appeared to Joseph Smith with golden tablets that contained another testament from God. It chronicled the history of the lost ten tribes of Israel in the Americas, including Christ's appearance in the Americas after his resurrection. God gave Smith the ability to translate the tablets, and then the angel took them back after he was finished. Smith's text is called the *Book of Mormon.*

On June 27, Joseph Smith was murdered. A scramble occurred to fill the leadership gap. Brigham Young was seen to be the likely candidate, but Strang produced a letter which he claimed was from Smith himself, proclaiming Strang as his successor! The letter was dated June 19 and seemed to be signed by Joseph Smith. Strang's claim created a schism within the council, resulting in the Mormons breaking into several groups. The majority followed Young, but another group followed Strang, and several other smaller groups also formed. They all departed for different regions of the country.

Brigham Young went west. James Strang went to Voree, Wisconsin. He then began to search for other places they could migrate to. He settled on the Beaver Island archipelago in northern Lake Michigan. Strang decided this would be the place to establish a Mormon colony. Soon, his followers came with him. He immediately claimed the Beaver Islands as Mormon possessions and declared the Mormons owed no allegiance to anyone but themselves. Quite a few non-Mormons, referred to as Gentiles, already inhabited the island, but they were ready to accept the Mormons in a live-and-let-live attitude.

The Mormons built a village on Beaver Island they named St. James. It still exists as a thriving community today. From there, Strang would rule his kingdom. One thing about Strang, he was smart. He was an intellectual of the highest degree—Strang was able to debate the most learned men of the time and stand toe-to-toe with them. Like Smith before him, he established a council of twelve disciples. They were Strang's lieutenants, and each had considerable power within the community. In the beginning, life was reasonably idyllic, but that began to change quickly.

In her memoir, *A Child of the Sea and My Life Among the Mormons*, Elizabeth Whitney Williams, who lived among the Mormons as a child, describes the changes:

> Strang claimed to have had several new revelations which must be told to his people. They all prepared for a great feast showing their joy. It would seem in his talk to them about his new revelations that he told them God was sending many Gentiles to be a help and a support to God's people, meaning themselves, the Latter Day Saints, and that it was right for his people to take whatever was necessary for them to have. That it was their privilege to take from the Gentiles. This was the first time that the King had openly given any orders of that nature to his people. Whether any Gentile had ever been admitted within the council room was never known, or whether some of his own people told what had been said, which many of us thought might be the case, but the news soon spread, and from that time no Gentile felt secure about his property. My father once asked Strang if he had ever preached to his people and given such orders. He answered he had not, but their actions soon told what their instructions had been.
>
> His people began to take from the Gentiles whatever they could get. Up to this time the feeling between the Mormons and Gentiles had been very friendly, the fishermen being glad to have the island settled with a good peaceful people as they had until now seemed to be. Mr. Peter McKinley at the Point was now suffering considerable losses by the Mormons taking his cattle and butchering them, also other goods which they were taking. A young man, or boy, Wheelock by name, told or gave information about the butchering of the cattle. He being a Mormon boy employed by Mr. McKinley, had to suffer the penalty by receiving fifty stripes with the 'Blue

Beeches,' that being one kind of their punishments. The boy had told the truth and had to suffer the cruel whipping.

Strang was seen as a prophet. He published pamphlets, from a print house set up in St. James, expounding his religious views and messages given to him by God. In one of these treatises, he speaks about how God told him the islands of the Great Lakes and the lands around them belonged to the chosen ones, the Mormons. Strang believed this and made his followers believe it. His followers claimed that Strang's was the only valid government on earth. More and more Mormons were flocking to Beaver Island, and Strang had them building a town and ships. What they didn't build they stole. Mormons with guns and knives would patrol Beaver Island, frightening those who weren't Mormon. They would walk into a house unannounced, sit down, and stay whenever they wanted to. If anyone complained, they would be beaten or killed. The Mormons continuously looted the Gentiles of their belongings, including fish, fishing boats, and nets. Most lived in continuous fear. When the Mormons killed a couple of the Gentiles, the fear became very real.

Eventually, all of the Gentiles were driven from Beaver Island. They were given ten days to convert to Mormonism or get out. Most got out, and many moved to the Charlevoix, Michigan area. The Beaver Island archipelago consists of seven islands, including Beaver Island itself. The Mormons now claimed all of them. The entire region of Lake Michigan now became deadly waters.

Newspapers reported that Strang had acquired three ships, the *Dolphin, Emmlin,* and *Seaman.* Thus began his pirate navy. Many ships that sailed into Mormon waters were captured, their cargos looted, and crews killed. Often, ships were simply burned so no evidence remained of the crime.

This eyewitness account from the Oswego Palladium tells a tale of a ship that sailed into Mormon water during a storm.

"On the east shore of Lake Michigan were fellows who pretended to follow fishing for a living; but who made more by luring vessels on to the beach by false lights and robbing vessels and crews than they did by their nets and hooks.

"For several years the followers of Joe Smith, the Mormon, lived on Beaver Island, Lake Michigan, and several vessels disappeared in that vicinity in mid-summer and neither they nor their crews were ever heard from. It was said that the Mormons boarded becalmed vessels, murdered the crews, discharged the cargoes on the island and burned or scuttled the craft. Iron of a kind that could only have been of use on board vessels, pork and beef barrelheads of a brand that Mormons never bought were found on the island by sailors and although an effort was made to ferret out the crimes, nothing ever came of it.

In the fall of 1849, I was fore-the-mast in a little brig belonging to Buffalo. She was trim little thing. She would serve as a yawl for the big hulks of today, clean and smart but as wet as a muskrat in springtime. As we neared the Beavers on our passage to Buffalo from Chicago, we caught it stiff and hard from the northward and the Captain thought he could breast out the breeze. He found when we worked abreast of the island that the seas were too 'lumpy' for our duck, as she was making dives that would do credit to a loon. It was late in the afternoon, well on towards nightfall, and, as the sky threatened snow, if the wind held the Captain concluded to go under the Beavers and let go our 'mud hooks' (anchors) until the storm had spent its fury.

We made our lee, luffed the brig up into the eye of the wind, let go both anchors, paid out the chain and soon the little brig was brought to a halt. After the canvas was furled, anchor watches were appointed and the rest of the crew turned in. About eight bells, midnight, Jack Stevens, who was on watch, shouted so loud that had we been mummies instead of men he must have awakened us. We did not scramble out very lively until the mate came to the scuttle and sang out 'Tumble up here , you beef eating, lazy dogs. We thought Jack had fallen asleep and tumbled off the forecastle deck and was frightened. When we heard the mate, a big brawny fellow, with a fist like a sledge hammer, we turned out mighty smart.

On reaching the deck we could see by the lights of the Mormon's houses that the brig was drifting fast towards the beach. A couple of smart fellows ran nimbly up the fore rigging, and quicker than thought, cast the gaskets off the topsail and as the buntlines and clewlines had been let go on deck, rode down the topsail halyards till the yardarm was as high as the double reef which had been tied outside , would permit the yardarm to go.

The jib was hoisted, as also was the peak of the mainsail, and when the canvas filled, the brig picked up her feet and clawed off the shore. The cause of the brig dragging was plain to be seen as soon as the matter was investigated. Both chains from the windlass to the hawser pipes were, instead of being taut as they should have been had the anchors been at the end, lying on the deck. When we pulled in-board the ends of the chain we found that both chains had been cut not far from the bow with a steel saw-cut as clean and slick as though the links had been held in a vise.

It was evident that the Mormons had been at work and had it not been for the timely discovery of Jack Stevens we would soon have been ashore and murdered. We stood off and on until morning and then the Captain hove to, lowered the yawl and went ashore to pry about and find the anchor if possible. He said nothing, he saw by the faces of the 'Latter Day Saints' that they were disappointed at the turn things had taken on the brig.

The brig never recovered the anchors and soon after the Captain returned, we sailed away. The next season while on a schooner from Ashtabula, I saw the same two anchors the brig lost the season before at the Beavers. I spoke to the Captain about it and he told me that he bought the anchors from the Mormons that spring. How did I know the anchors? I knew them by the marks Tom Jones, a shipmate, made while sitting on them spinning yarns. Tom was a bouncing big fellow and he sat on the anchors so much that he marked them with hearts."

Eventually, Strang sent his ships out on raiding trips. They painted the sails black and came in the dead of night. Any village along the Lake Michigan coast was at peril of an attack by the Mormon pirates. They took everything. Food, tools, livestock—anything usable—became the booty of Strang's Mormon pirates. They also tried to set up a colony at Charlevoix, but a fierce gun battle ensued and Strang's Mormons were driven off.

Like Joseph Smith before him, Strang claimed a Mormon kingdom. He had a ceremony and crowned himself king! As luck would have it, one of the newly arrived Mormons was a Shakespearean actor complete with a Hamlet costume. Strang took advantage of the opportunity to dress as Hamlet for the coronation. He claimed Beaver Island was a Mormon Kingdom, and with his printing house, he started producing his own money. The US Government was not amused.

Then Strang changed, becoming inconsistent. When he first established the colony, he had only allowed monogamy. Now he began to take wives. His first and true wife packed up her three children and immediately left. Polygamy didn't sit well with many of his followers. There was a lot of grumbling. Plots began to develop. One plot is described by Charles J. Strang for the *New York Times*.

> Bloody collisions were not infrequent and finally became a murderous one. The Mormons were well provided with pistols and muskets and were the proprietors of a small cannon. They also had boats of their own. In 1850 the fishermen planned a Fourth of July celebration at Beaver Island, which was to reach a patriotic climax in the forcible expulsion of the Mormons, but the firing of a national salute from a shotted cannon and the parade of armed Saints in large numbers brought that project to an inglorious termination.

It was obvious that Strang's Mormons were wreaking havoc on Lake Michigan. Ships and crews were disappearing and something had to be done. Unfettered crime under the guise of God was wearing thin.

A headline and article from the Allegan Record goes like this:

Wholesale Robbery by Pirates on Lake Michigan!

The people along Lake Michigan, from here north to the Manitous, have been thrown into a state of the most intense excitement by the operations of a gang of marauders, who are reported to be Mormons from Beaver Island, and who have carried on their operations with a boldness, coolness, and desperation rarely equaled in the records of highwaymen.

They are reported to have burned sawmills and robbed stores north of the Grand River. At Grand Haven they made repeated attempts to break into stores and shops. On Saturday of last week they made their appearance at the mouth of the Kalamazoo, and after looking about, pushed up south as far as the tanneries in the town of Ganges, and on Saturday night broke open Robinson and Plummer's store, robbing them of $1600 worth of goods, and made back again down the lake.

Off Port Sheldon, they were seen by a vessel's crew anchored there, with their plunder all open to view, and were pulling on down as carelessly and fearlessly as though they were pursuing a legitimate calling. There is said to be upwards of twenty in the gang. They sail one small schooner of twenty or thirty tons and two Mackinaw boats.

Robinson and Plummer pursued them as far north as Grand Haven and then turned back the people advising them that it would be useless and unsafe to pursue them further without a strong force of men. What is to be done in the premises we do not hear. Surely we have come upon strange times, if such high-handed robberies can be perpetrated and go unwhipped of justice. There seems to be no question as to the identity of the robbers and their hiding place. They are emissaries from King Strang's realms, and the whole power of the state should be lent to ferret out and bring to justice the perpetrators of such bold crimes.

President Millard Fillmore ordered the U.S. District Attorney, George Bates to dig into Strang and his followers. Strang suddenly found himself accused of treason, theft, and counterfeiting. They even threw in trespassing on government land for good measure. Strang was then dragged to Detroit in 1851 to be tried (other sources say it was Mackinac Island). At the trial, Strang chose to defend himself. He blamed the government's accusations on ignorance and persecution. His eloquence won him the trial. It also made him some new enemies. His public image was getting favorable press after the trial, which irked anti-Mormons.

In 1853, Strang decided to run for the Michigan State House of Representatives as a Democrat. Again, he won. As he went to take his seat in the legislature, the anti-Strang members tried to deny him his seat. Speaking before the legislature, Strang pressed his case with such a deft ability at oratory that most came around to his side and he was allowed to take his seat.

Strang represented what was formerly Manitou County, which consisted of Beaver Island and its surrounding islands, together with the North and South Manitou Islands and Fox Islands in Lake Michigan. The county existed from 1855 to 1895, after which it was absorbed into present-day Emmett County. The Manitou County seat was at St. James on Beaver Island. In his time in the legislature, Strang authored and passed fifteen bills. He was well liked by his non-Mormon constituents and was even reelected for a second term. Although it should be mentioned that the Mormon population was a large voting block that he controlled completely.

Strang was able to get lighthouses erected on Beaver Island. These marked the Beaver Island locations so sailors could safely sail around them, or so it was intended. The pirates made use of them in another way, wrecking. *Mooncussing* or wrecking was a common ploy on the Great Lakes, as it was elsewhere. The concept is simple: The official light in the lighthouse is extinguished and a fire is set on shore in a different location. A passing ship will think the fire is the lighthouse and the end result is usually the ship runs up on a rock shoal. The waiting pirates or wreckers will board the ship, kill the crew, and take the cargo. Beaver Island and the surrounding islands were now one big trap.

An old unnamed sailor from this time recalled:

> Old Strang was a bad one. One time there was a fine schooner anchored down here in Sand Bay to wait out a blow. She was a fine new schooner and when it came dark them Mormons came down on her and murdered the whole crew except the two daughters of the captain who were making the trip with him. Strang sees them and has them put in his boat and struck for the harbor with them but on the way one of the girls jumps overboard and they think she has drowned and went on but she swam back to the schooner and got a hold of the bob stays and there she was a hanging when two Irishmen seeing the schooner and thinking she might be in trouble, rowed out and found the girl exhausted. She told them her story and they took her back with them. One of the men was married and his wife took care of her and the fellow who wasn't married went to the nearest Mormon house and with two loaded pistols, stole a horse and rode as fast as it could run right up to Strang's big palace and went in and made them all put up their hands except the girl who he told to go out and get on the horse and as soon as she did he backed out still keeping their hands up. There was old Strang and his five wives and some others and he got out and on the horse and rode with the girl.

When Strang was displeased or he perceived some infraction, he would have the perpetrator publicly flogged. One such individual, who had been given a beating of seventy-five lashes with beech branches was Thomas Bedford, who swore he would get revenge for the public humiliation. He had been accused of giving information about Mormon thefts, but there was never any evidence he had betrayed them and his denials went unheard.

On June 16, 1856, Bedford took his revenge along with another Strangite named Wentworth who had also been punished by Strang. It was late at night, and the *USS Michigan* lay quietly in the harbor.

Thomas Bedford, one of James Jesse Strang's Assassins

Captain Alexander St. Bernard, who was a mate at the time, gives an eyewitness account of the assassination:

> I was an officer on the United States Steamer *Michigan* for twenty-five years. She was the first iron boat that navigated the lakes. We generally took on wood at Beaver Island. There were between two thousand and three thousand Mormons living there then, with their leader King Strang, besides the Gentiles who were mostly fishermen and woodcutters. The Mormons lived in houses of hewn logs and worshipped in a large temple built of the same material, which they also used for a theater and dance hall. There was a platform across one end with scenery at the back, a movable pulpit, which was built on trucks. It was a queer affair, a sort of circular platform, with seats around the outside edge for the twelve apostles and a high seat in the center for the king. When they had a show of any kind the pulpit was rolled behind the scenery, out of sight.
>
> I was well acquainted with the king, for he often came on board the ship. He was a fine looking, sociable sort of a man, but he was not very popular among the Gentiles. We heard a great many complaints from them whenever we stopped there. The Mormons were obliged to turn over one-tenth of their earnings to the king and he demanded the same from the Gentiles. Two fishermen, who refused to surrender their hard-earned money, were taken to the woods, stripped and beaten with beech switches and the county treasurer, who lived on the island, was ordered to deliver up one-tenth of the public money.
>
> When we stopped as usual on one of our trips around the lakes, the complaints were so bitter that our captain made up his mind to arrest him [Strang] again, and he told me to find him and bring him on board the ship. I went to the temple first, where I was told that he had just gone home. I found him sitting in his room, with four of his wives, where he received me very cordially and when I told him of my errand, accompanied me willingly. He linked arms with me and we

walked along talking pleasantly. Just as we stepped on the dock and started to walk down the narrow passage between the piles of wood, two of his enemies sprang from some hiding place and shot at him. He clung to my arm until they began to pound him with the butt of their pistols, when he let go and fell, leaving me covered with blood from my head to my feet.

The news spread in a very short time and a howling mob of men, women, and children gathered around their dying chief. Our surgeon came onshore and did what he could for the poor fellow, but nothing could save him. He died in the arms of his first and real wife, whose home was west of Racine, in Wisconsin.

The murderers ran aboard the ship and gave themselves up, the best thing they could have done, for the mob would have pulled them in pieces if they had caught them. Of course, suspicion fell on me, many thinking I had led him to his death and I received several friendly warnings to be on my guard, but I was not molested. A detachment of troops were sent to bring the fishermen and their families on board the ship as it was considered unsafe to leave them on the island with the excited Mormons.

The murderers were taken to Mackinac and given into the custody of the county sheriff, Mr. Granger, who kept the Grove House at that time, but they were never brought to trial.

Of course, suspicion and conspiracy theories run rampant about King Strang's demise. Even the account above has the narrator not lifting a finger to do anything to ward off the attackers even when they are beating him. The *USS Michigan* sitting conveniently in the harbor for the murderers to get away seemed a little too coincidental for many. The captain of the *Michigan*, Captain McBlair, was accused of being a part of the assassination plot, but there was no evidence to prove the theory.

Strang was shot three times. On bullet grazed his head while another hit him in the cheek. The third shot hit him in the spine,

USS *Michigan* under sail and steam in the Strang era

immediately paralyzing him below the waist. Strang hung on to life for nearly three weeks. He was transported back to Voree, Wisconsin, where he was bedridden until his death. He was cared for by his first wife. He died on July 9, 1856. He was forty-three.

The assassins, Bedford and Wentworth, were taken to Mackinac Island. The captain of the *Michigan* refused to turn them over to the local sheriff at Manitou County since he was Mormon. Instead, he gave them to the sheriff at Mackinac. The assassins were hailed for ridding Lake Michigan of a nuisance more than they were reviled as murderers. Reports say that their cells were never locked, and when a trial was held, it was a mere formality with a foregone conclusion. The two men were released. One source says they were both fined $1.25, while other sources say they just walked free, much to the happiness of the local citizens. No more Strang, no more raids.

Hearing of the assassination attempt, a group of non-Mormons gathered at a small village on St. Helena Island. People came from surrounding communities from Mackinac to Cheboygan, tired of having been raided by Strang's pirates. A fleet of ships set out for Beaver Island. In a night of absolute terror, the ships' crews swept down on the island with fury and vengeance. The Mormons were told to leave everything behind and board the ships that the fleet had brought with them. If they refused, they were shot and/or beaten. All of their belongings were left behind, including caches of money. This incident has led over the years to rumors and tales of Mormon money buried around Beaver Island. Cleansed from the island, the Mormons on the ships were unceremoniously dropped off at ports around Lake Michigan in places like Cheboygan, Frankfort, and Grand Haven. It was the end of a wild and ruthless time on the northern waters of Lake Michigan.

The Legend of King Strang's Treasure

This is a story without documentation, yet throughout the years the tale has persisted. Where did all of King Strang's money go? He had amassed a large fortune through Mormon tithes and revenue from all of the goods they stole. He was known to store it inside his home on Beaver Island in a brass box. When Strang was shot, he was carried to a nearby house. Realizing that this might be the end for the Mormon King, the box of money was removed from his house within an hour.

The box was transported to the west side of Beaver Island. With Strang out of the way, it didn't take a lot of figuring to realize that this was probably the end of the Mormon colony. One of Strang's followers then took the brass box to High Island, a five mile row in a small boat. By comparison, that would be equivalent to rowing from Mackinaw City to St. Ignace.

Once on High Island, the box was taken inland to where a great tree stood. Thirty paces from the tree the brass box was buried. No indication of the direction of travel was reported. This final movement of the treasure happened in a single night and the perpetrator was back before dawn. There has been no record of its recovery.

In the search for the brass box, High Island was logged and thus most of the big trees were harvested removing the location's landmark. Beginning in 1912, High Island was home to the House of David group, commonly known as the High Island Cult. They had a colony on High Island for many years where they cultivated much of the island's acreage. Eventually, the weather drove them out and they abandoned the buildings and colony completely in 1927. Following the Armistice Blizzard of 1940, Odawa fishermen moved from Beaver Island to High Island.

The state of Michigan officially acquired the majority of High Island in 1958 using Pittman-Robertson Funds to preserve it as public wilderness. As such, state law prohibits the removal of any items from state land and if the treasure were discovered the State would certainly step in and demand possession.

Mormon records make no mention of the fate of Strang's treasury. Most likely it found its way back to Voree and went into the coffers there.

5   Piracy During the American Civil War

Johnson's Island Prison (sketch)

During the Civil War, the Great Lakes was a hot spot of activity. We normally think of the Civil War as having been fought in the southern United States, but its effects were much more far reaching. The St. Lawrence Seaway wasn't seen as under threat, so it followed that the Great Lakes were considered the same.

Consequently, only one ship patrolled the Great Lakes, at the time, the *USS Michigan*. It would patrol the Great Lakes on what seemed like easy duty. As the war raged on, a prison camp was established on Johnson's Island offshore of Sandusky, Ohio, in Lake

Erie for what would eventually hold thousands of Confederate prisoners.

There were many Southern sympathizers in the North and Canada. Not everyone was on board with the Union's side of the Civil War. Beginning in 1863, a plan was developed by Canadian sympathizers to hijack the *USS Michigan*, kill the crew, and then sail it to Johnson's Island to free the ever-growing number of POWs there. A Confederate naval crew was picked to sail the *Michigan* once it was overwhelmed. As the only gunboat in the region, the *Michigan* would be hard to stop. As the plot was about to unfold, Confederate President Jefferson Davis stopped the plan.

That was only the beginning. The plan kept being kicked around. One plot had twenty-two rebels travel to Nova Scotia where they hooked up with thirty-two more escaped prisoners. A message was smuggled into Johnson's Island, warning the prisoners of the impending attack and to be prepared. They booked passage on a steamer to Chicago, where the *Michigan* was docked. Unfortunately, the Canadian Government got wind of it and warned the US of the attack.

USS Michigan crewman William Baas served in the Civil War era

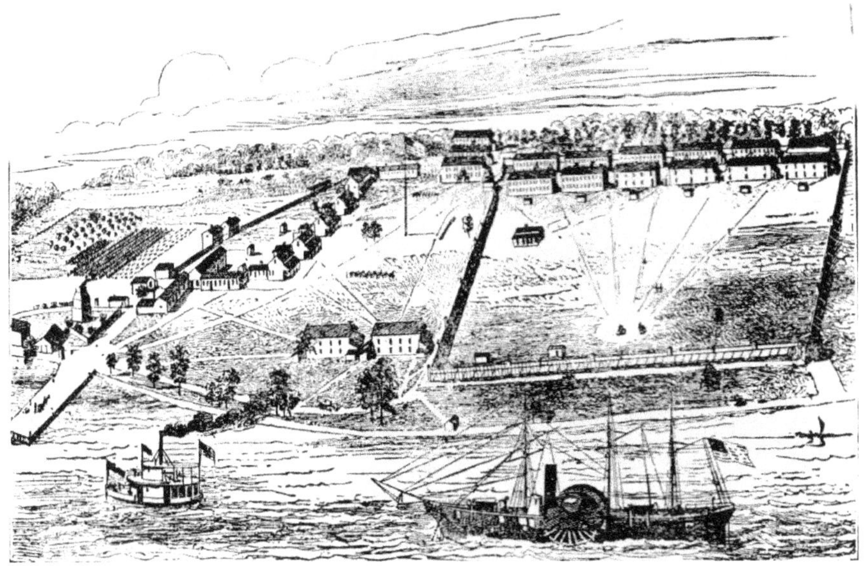

Lithograph of Johnson's Island with *USS Michigan*.
(Edward Gould, Company B, 128th Ohio)

One year later, another plot hatched, this time with one of the Confederates, Charles Cole, claiming to be able to ingratiate himself to the crew of the *Michigan* and get them drunk or drug them. After that, a steamer would come alongside and take over the ship while the crew was intoxicated or passed out. They would then take the *Michigan* and release the prisoners from Johnson's Island, dropping them ashore where they would create havoc far behind enemy lines as they worked their way home.

Jack Carter, the captain of the *Michigan*, seemed to know something was in the wind. Rumors of a plot brewing to capture the *Michigan* had reached his ears. He called to his cabin a bright and promising young soldier named John Murray. Captain Carter sent Murray on a secret mission to find out if the rumors were true and send word back to the Captain whatever he found out.

Murray went on a search for Confederate sympathizers, first in Detroit and then across the Detroit River to Windsor. There he came across a Copperhead (southern sympathy group) organizer named Vallandigham who was residing in Canada because his views didn't set well in Ohio. At the time, there were many rumors of a Northwest Confederacy being formed. Murray eavesdropped on a conversation between Vallandigham and a man of seeming importance, it turned out to be Charles Cole! Convinced that Cole was up to something. Murray began following him. First he went to Toledo, where Cole met with several southern sympathizers.

Later, to Montreal where Cole picked up a woman accomplice. Murray describes her.

> She was an elegant looking lady. She was big and stately, a magnificent blonde with clothes that were a marvel to me. I did not know her then, but later she turned out to be the celebrated Irish Lize. The contrast between her and Cole was striking. She was big, stout, and fine looking; he was a little sandy, redhaired fellow, but smart as lightning.

Now travelling together, Cole and Irish Lize (a.k.a. Annie Cole, Anna Brown, Annie Davis, and Belle Brandon) began recruiting men to join their plot. They went to Albany, Philadelphia, Washington, Buffalo, Cleveland… anywhere they could find a sympathetic ear, thus laying the groundwork for their plot. All the while Murray followed them.

In Cleveland, Cole and Lize posed as man and wife and met with a new conspirator, John Yates Beall. Beall had approached the Confederacy to make him a privateer in the Great Lakes. He was turned down, but when he heard of the plot against the *Michigan*, he volunteered to lead the raid. Beall was the man selected to lead the assault from Canada and board the *Michigan* with the men to take it over. The pieces were nearly in place, the piracy of the *Michigan* could begin.

In September of 1864 the plot unfolded. Cole was very personable and became friends with the officers of Johnson's Island and the *Michigan*. He treated them lavishly with cigars and liquor. On the night of the hijacking, the story varies here, Cole set up a dinner for the officers of the *Michigan*. One account says this was to happen onshore in Sandusky while another source says the dinner was on the *Michigan* itself. Cole intended for the officers to become drunk or drugged.

Rare photo of USS Michigan crew and mid-deck

Unfortunately, thanks to Murray and a soldier at Johnson's island that had overheard the plot, Captain Carter was aware of Cole's plan. Cole offered them liquor and a huge bribe of $50,000 to let him go free. They were having none of it and threw Charles Cole into the brig.

In the meantime, Beall and the Confederates had stolen a steamer named the *Philo Parsons*. It travelled around Canada picking up somewhere between 18 and 25 men, each bearing a single trunk of luggage—these were filled with weapons.

One account shows how Beall took the *Philo Parsons*. "After the steamer Parsons got well into Lake Erie, these men opened their luggage boxes, took therefrom braces of revolvers and captured the Parsons, making her captain prisoner." Buell then had the Confederate flag raised over the Philo Parsons. It is the only time the flag of the Confederacy has flown on the Great Lakes.

Cole was supposed to fire a signal to give the all clear that the crew had been taken care of, which he failed to do. Without the signal, those on the *Philo Parsons* knew that Cole had failed and they

The *Philo Parsons*, pirated by Confederates

turned back. Many of the men becoming paranoid that they had been found out. The *Philo Parsons* was actually in sight of the *Michigan* when it turned around! The captain of the *Michigan* waited for the planned attack, thinking he'd set a trap for them, but he began to realize that it wasn't going to be sprung.

Running low on fuel, the *Philo Parsons* steamed to Bass Island where the Confederates knew they could get cordwood. Under the command of Beall, they began to load on cordwood. The captain of another ship, the *Island Queen*, had the same idea and pulled in alongside the *Philo Parsons*. The *Island Queen* threw ropes to tie up to the *Philo Parsons*, but men on the *Parsons* refused to take them. Several of the crew jumped aboard to tie the ropes and the Confederates on the *Parsons* pulled their guns. The boat had several Union soldiers aboard but they were all unarmed. The soldiers were on shore leave, but Beall and several of his men let their paranoia get the best of them and believed that the soldiers were after the *Philo Parsons*, that the union had somehow found out about their plot and had sent the soldiers after them, so he had his men fire on them and took them prisoners.

One of the soldiers recounts the story,

> The Queen arrived about 6 o'clock and we boarded her for Toledo, but she had to stop at Middle Bass Island for fuel wood. Capt. Orr of the *Island Queen*, when near the dock, saw the *Philo Parsons* laying at the dock and running alongside of her tried to put a line aboard the Parsons but no one

would take the lines, so some of the crew of the *Queen* jumped aboard the *Parsons* and fastened the lines and were promptly seized and placed under guard. Captain Buell in command of the Confederates, finding the soldiers were unarmed, boarded the *Island Queen* and rounded them up and put them in the hold of the Parsons.

Captain Orr of the *Queen* mistrusted something was wrong after the crew of the *Parsons* refused to take his lines, rang the 'go ahead bell' and, getting no results went aft to see what the trouble was and was promptly captured. The men on guard in the engine room of the *Queen* when the engineer attempted to obey the signal to go ahead, shot him through the face. (It was not fatal and he afterward recovered.)

After being in the hold of the *Parsons* for an hour or so we were taken on deck and were paroled under promise not to leave the island for twenty-four hours. The *Philo Parsons* then took the *Island Queen* in tow and, after getting clear of Ballast Island, scuttled her. There was no one injured aboard the *Philo Parsons*, when captured by the Confederates, and on the *Island Queen* there was but one shot fired, at the engineer as noted above. However, they used hatchets freely on the heads of soldiers, but no one was seriously injured."

Having no room on the *Philo Parsons*, they left the Union soldiers on Bass Island and sailed up the Detroit River. The Confederates abandoned the steamship on the shore after stripping and looting the ship.

John Murray comments on the Confederate plot:

They had all of their plans made to meet Cole and go in small boats to the Michigan, capture the ship, and then run over to Johnson's Island and release the four thousand Confederate prisoners, chiefly officers, imprisoned there. They planned to land them in Point Pelee in Canada, right across the lake. They were to approach the Michigan, and when asked who came there Cole would answer. He was well known to all, and relied on no one to suspect him. Once aboard, he believed he could carry the hatches with a rush. The Michigan had fourteen cannon aboard her, six parrot rifles, six twenty-four pound howitzers, two light howitzers, and over a hundred tons of ammunition. They had no other heavily armed craft to fear on the lake. They believed they could not only liberate their four thousand men on Johnson's Island and land them in Canada, but also could sail the lake without fear of superior vessel until they bombarded and burned Detroit, Cleveland, and Buffalo. Some of the captured papers corroborated details of this plot.

John Murray would go on to be an amateur sleuth. Charles Cole would be pardoned by President Lincoln on March 10, 1865, barely a month for Lincoln's eventual assassination. Irish Lize was arrested but her fate is unknown. John Yates Buell hanged on February 24, 1865, at Fort Columbus on Governors Island.

The Confederates would try one more time in 1864. This fourth plot featured a ship called the *Georgian*, which the Confederacy had purchased from Canada. The intent was to use the 130-foot steamer to attack cities and capture and destroy Union ships. The *Georgian* was armed, and it was also ordered to free Johnson's Island's prisoners. Fear of the *Georgian* was fueled by Southern newspapers and Confederate sympathizers, creating almost a state of panic in the North. The City of Buffalo was worried enough that it brought out two cannons and mounted them on tugs. Eventually, the *Georgian* was run down by the *Michigan* and searched, but the crew found nothing to hold them on. When the *Georgian* was put up for the winter, a spy the Union had slipped onboard learned that the Confederates were mounting a battering ram onto the front of the ship. When the Union complained to Canada, Canada turned the *Georgian* over to the Union, killing the project and driving a nail into the South's coffin.

The Confederates were arguably the most incompetent pirates ever.

USS *Michigan* as she appeared during the Civil War era (1860)

6   What About Lost Pirate Treasure?

First, a word about Civil War gold and other lost treasures. Stories abound of lost pirate gold, but none of the Great Lakes pirates actually buried their treasures with the exception of the Apostle Pirates and Strang and the Mormons. Instead, these pirates simply spent their bounties. Although gold was shipped through the Caribbean, the targets of Great Lakes piracy were merely commodities to be resold. Consequently, their stolen cargoes would never have brought them a fortune.

Quite a few stories are told of gold being smuggled out of the South through the Great Lakes. These stories have nothing to do with pirates but with failed attempts to financially revive the Southern cause. Most Civil War gold stories are stories of failure; hence, a treasure awaits the one lucky enough to come across it.

As the South began to lose the war, different plans were presented to get the Confederate treasury out of danger from capture by the Union. One of the ideas was to bring it through the Great Lakes and then down from the North into Texas or Missouri to revive the Southern cause. Some stories claimed this happened and that some of the ships sailing the Great Lakes carried Confederate gold.

One of the most famous of those treasures is supposed to be near Poverty Island, twelve miles south of the Garden Peninsula in Lake Michigan. The story goes, when the Civil War was becoming an obvious lost cause, a desperate call for financing went out to France. Emperor Napoleon III supposedly secretly sent a large shipment of gold, roughly $400 million, to Canada in 1863. Of course, Canada has always had strong ties to the French, so getting someone to work with the Emperor would not have been difficult. The gold was then sailed down the St. Lawrence River and eventually into Lake Michigan. Here's where the story gets murky. Some believe the ship was attacked and sunk while many believe there was a storm that sent her to the bottom. Either way, it has become the stuff of legends, and it is believed that the treasure lies off the Garden Peninsula near Poverty Island. Today, treasure hunters search for it on a regular basis.

Another legend of lost gold and hidden treasure was the story that the Incas or Aztecs made their way north, fleeing the Spanish, carrying a huge treasure of gold. It was rumored that these Indians came up the Mississippi and into Lake Superior, eventually hiding their gold somewhere around Little Girl's Point on Lake Superior. One of the early residents of Little Girl's Point, George Triplett, took this legend seriously.

Triplett began digging all around the Little Girl's Point area, prospecting. The region had long been considered worthless for commercial mining. He dug one pit after another, some 80 to 100 feet deep. Triplett was closed-mouthed about what he found, which added to the rumors and speculation. Triplett found silver and copper and hinted at possibly other things. He was even able to use the story of lost Indian treasure to get some investors. For years he dug, but if the lost treasure was there, he never found it.

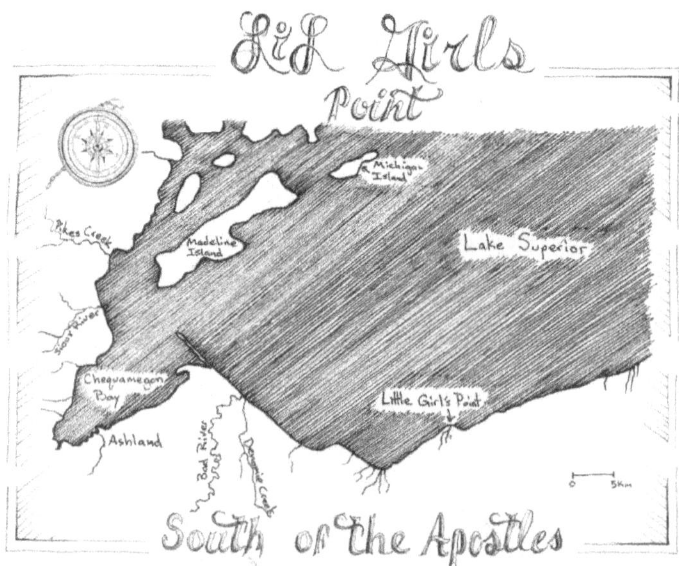

7 Timber Pirates and Other Piracy

In the 1800s, much of Michigan and Wisconsin was owned by the federal government. Timber harvesting was illegal on most of these public lands without a permit. The great white pines were in high demand. The feds wanted the wood for building a navy to prepare for the Civil War, and the public wanted the wood for building and the land cleared for agriculture. The result was timber pirates and the Timber Rebellion of 1853.

The timber pirates would slip into a place. Cut down a "40" (forty acres) of the trees, and then quickly load them onto ships, and sail away to a port to sell their contraband lumber. Many of these pirates were subsidized and even employed by legitimate and "respectable" lumber companies. Surprisingly, the public was on the side of the timber pirates because they saw the forest and wilderness as impeding the progress of civilization. When the feds went to enforce the timber laws, the locals would often rise up and free the guilty parties.

In 1851, the federal government sent out Timber Agents associated with the Department of the Interior. This did not set well. Local papers, such as the *Chicago Tribune* and the *Chicago Democratic Press*, clamored for armed resistance against the timber agents, saying, "If they regard their personal welfare, they had better keep clear of such transactions as that which they are about to engage in. If men cannot have a law to protect their personal property, they will protect it themselves." Protests against the timber

USS *Michigan* in 1930s

agents grew, even coming down to a public log burning at Grand Haven, Michigan, as a mock "Boston Tea Party."

As was often the case, the *Michigan* was on duty in the Lakes and was ordered to help keep the peace and enforce the timber laws. In 1853, as the *Michigan* was sailing Lake Huron's southern portion, one of the officers spotted a light ahead. The helmsman was ordered to avoid it. The light kept moving ahead of the ship. The *Michigan* closed in on the light, which now had been identified as a large steamer named the *Buffalo*. As they closed in on each other, the steamer suddenly made a ninety-degree turn and rammed the bow of the *Michigan*. It caused a lot of damage.

Because the *Michigan* was an ironclad, the hull held and didn't leak. The *Michigan* wouldn't sink. The steamer just bounced off, and the captain immediately turned his ship and sailed away. The *Michigan* didn't pursue but headed to Chicago to repair the damages. On the way, the captain filed a protest against the *Buffalo* at Mackinac Island. In Chicago, the *Michigan* was laid up for a month for repairs. At first the captain Charles H. McBlair of the

Michigan thought the ramming was accidental, but on reflection decided they had hit the Michigan on purpose.

When the *Michigan* returned to the water, they once again began their interdiction of the timber pirates. Several arrests were made, but when it came time for prosecution and trial, the prisoners were either not prosecuted or acquitted. Everything seemed to be for naught.

In 1877, President Hayes appointed Carl Shurz as Secretary of the Treasury. He went to work prosecuting anyone who was involved in the timber thefts on public lands. He unseated corrupt officials and replaced them. He sent out agents to enforce the laws against lumber barons and got the funding for enforcement. This spelled the end of the timber pirates. Unfortunately, great damage had been done to the forests of the Great Lakes, making the actions almost moot.

Random Acts of Piracy

There were also random acts of piracy such as in this story from the *Detroit Post and Tribune* in 1877:

> The gang of pirates that have been committing depredations the whole length of the Detroit and St. Clair Rivers have got a check put on their operations for a while. A black sloop scow about 40 feet long by 12 feet wide with a covered cabin 10 feet wide by 16 feet long and 5 feet high that had been seen lying along the shores at different times, was suspicioned and a watch set over her doings. Last night she was captured, together with one able bodied seaman, and had there been less haste, the balance of the gang, together with their boats might have been captured. The man captured was lodged in jail and when the officer went to carry him a warm breakfast, behold the lockup had no doors on it. But the boat, which was a very nice new scow with a perfect outfit, is in charge where moths and rust will not injure or thieves yank her away. The boat has no name.

The *New York Times* reported a group of twenty pirates who were raiding communities on the west shore of Lake Michigan. They looted shops and torched sawmills, then would sail off into Lake Michigan. At one point, they were pursued by the law, but they still managed to escape.

The Sawmill Escapade

In 1890, there were four brothers of the Moile family: John, George, Henry, and James. They were from Saginaw, Michigan and set up a large sawmill in Detour, Michigan. The four brothers invested everything and carried a large debt. Unfortunately, they weren't able to secure enough logs to make the sawmill profitable even though they had been running a large logging operation. They were then lent even more money from a firm in Alpena. $70,000 more. It was looking like they would never be out from under debt's heavy load.

Henry Moiles, the less-than-honest lawyer in the family came up with an idea to save the company from their creditors. They would steal their own sawmill and take it to Canada! The brothers agreed and they began work to remove the equipment at spring ice breakup. They went back to their home in Saginaw and acquired a tug, named *Tom Dowling* and two barges to carry the equipment across the water. They brought them up Lake Huron. The Moiles brothers had used the excuse that they were bringing lumber back with them to lower Michigan after they had it milled.

Behind closed doors, men were at work dismantling every bit of the mill machinery. A story was spread that the mill equipment needed maintenance and they were disassembling some of it to be shipped for overhauling.

The financiers from Alpena were told this operation was for improvements to the mill. The lending firm even sent along a pair of watchmen to oversee the upgrades. The brothers managed to keep them away from the mill far enough they didn't catch on. Liquor worked for one and the other was called away on a false emergency. The brothers had hired someone to rush in and exclaim that the man's wife was having a baby. They then doctored the horse so it would get ill when the watchman was part way home. He had to walk five miles to his house to find his wife still fine and still pregnant.

With both watchmen out of the way, the brothers and their crew began loading every piece of the mill onto the barges. Engines, boilers, tramways, everything right down to and including the nails. They left nothing. The total value of the property left behind was less than five dollars. The entire project was finished loading by 1:30 a.m. The tug and barges moved out into the night. They were now pirates.

By dawn they had made about 7 miles. The drift ice was thick and the tug was having difficulty moving through them. By 4:30 p.m. they crossed the international boundary near Whiskey Point on St. Joseph Island. They were now in Canadian water and they felt safe.

Meanwhile, the watchman had returned to find everything gone. At this time the tug and barges were still in sight. He hastened to the telegraph office to contact his superiors in Alpena and send a message to Sheriff McKenzie at Sault Ste. Marie. Unfortunately, the wires had been cut. The Moile brothers had been very thorough.

The tug had now become ice-bound and wasn't moving at all. It was the second day and word had finally reached the sheriff. The watchman had made it to Pickford and put in a call. The sheriff put together a group of deputies and had a tug of his own. Accounts differ on whether the Sheriff came from the Sault or was forced to go to St. Ignace due to ice clogging the St. Mary's River. But, the result was he was headed for the Moiles.

John Moile was captain of the tug and saw the pursuit coming. As they gave chase, Moile became increasingly worried that the sheriff would be able to get a line on one of the barges and pull it back across the border. Moile grabbed a rifle and proceeded to the tug's stern. He shouted to the sheriff that if he attempted to board the tug or the barges, that he would drill such a hole in his body that his friends would be able to see next Christmas though it! Consequently, the sheriff was convinced while being unsure where the international boundary really was and well outnumbered by the Moiles and their crew. He turned back to the mainland.

The small fleet was locked into the spring ice for three days. An offshore wind kept them trapped. Finally, the wind shifted and they were able to make their way into Worsley Bay. Eventually they would reach their destination of Johns Island in Georgian Bay in northern Lake Huron. They had no trouble with Canadian customs, paid a duty of $6,000 and set up their mill at what is known today as Moiles Bay.

The brothers operated their mill for a few years before they were bought out by another milling company. The Alpena company that they owed the money to bought up much of the surrounding forest in Canada and refused to sell any of the wood to the Moiles. The brothers never did make much money running the sawmill and were grateful to get out.

Bill "Bully" Hayes

A more famous pirate, Captain William (Bully) Henry Hayes, got his start in the Great Lakes. Hayes became a notorious South Seas pirate after he left his home of Cleveland, Ohio. His career began by sailing the Great Lakes with his own ship. He built a reputation as a brawler who grew up in his father's saloon.

It was a rough beginning, but Hayes was fascinated by stories of the captains and sailors. It wasn't long before he was out on his own, getting what he could around Lake Erie. It is said by those who knew him:

> Bully Hayes would have fooled his jailer, taken tea with the Governor of the prison, asked the chaplain to pray for him, emptied the prison safe and then vamoosed with the Governor's daughter and what's more, he'd have dropped a donation into the poor box before leaving.

Hayes' escapades helped cement the reputation of Cleveland as a "hell-raising" town. An older resident of Cleveland comments "When Bill Hayes, the Pacific Pirate, sailed on the lakes, he was not the only one who could steal a vessel or lure one to a rock-bound coast."

Unfortunately, Hayes got caught up in a shady scheme and was accused of horse stealing. He had to leave the area. He eventually went to San Francisco and then the South Pacific. He built a reputation there that spanned the world. There were even dime novel stories written about Bully Hayes Buccaneer. He achieved a reputation as one of the best and cleverest sailors on the Pacific.

The Cleveland pirate's exploits in the South Pacific are well documented, though with the added mythology added by the novels, separating fact from fiction is difficult. Still, it proves that the Great Lakes was a good breeding ground for pirates.

Only known photo of Captain William ("Bully") Henry Hayes

Bully Hayes Buccaneer #5

Mackinac Island Post Office Robbery

The Headline read "Pirates Rob Mackinac Island Post Office." It all began in 1893 when a small sailboat carrying three men sailed into the Mackinac Island harbor. There was nothing unusual about that. The three of them quietly walked to the post office and broke in. They took everything of any value including postage stamps. The Pirates quietly sailed away in their boat, over $2000 richer.

A little background: at this time, Mackinac Island was the main post office. Little small town post offices hadn't been established, and Mackinac was the post office for all of the Upper Peninsula and Northern Lower Michigan. A person might get their mail a couple of times a year, not every day like now. The trio stole $959.98 in postage stamps, $1031.84 in postal funds, and $53.14 in money order funds.

A newspaper article picks up the story.

> *Pirates on the Lakes*! A gang of thieves is operating from a swift sailboat along the shores of Lake Michigan and the Straits of Mackinac. They are now being pursued by a tug with a regular detachment of soldiers from Fort Mackinac. They are well armed and a meeting is sure to result in bloodshed.
>
> The post office in Mackinac Island was looted Sunday night and over $2000 worth of stamps and money stolen. The work was evidently done by expert cracksmen. A few nights before the post office at Charlevoix had been broken into in a similar manner.
>
> On the night of the Mackinac Island robbery, a strange looking craft came to a landing and mysteriously disappeared in the morning. The officer's suspicions were immediately aroused. Lou Jaquette, James Murray, and William Donnelly chartered a tug and gave chase. After running 48 miles along the north shore west they came up to a sailboat and, recognizing the boat and the three men, ordered the latter to surrender.

The thieves at once opened fire. Murray was shot in the hand, while one of the yachtsmen received a bullet in the breast and fell. The fusillade continued for some time when the thieves surrendered. Two of them came on board, were bound and secured in the hold of the boat. An attempt was made to get the third one, who was hiding under a small deck in the bow of the sailboat. Jaquette exhausted all of his ammunition, when the robber came out and covered Jaquette and his crew with two large revolvers and demanded the release of his two partners.

The officers were at his mercy and the request was complied with. The two prisoners were released and the sailboat cut adrift. The tug returned to Mackinac Island for reinforcements, and a detachment of soldiers from the fort, with several officers, on board the steamer North Star, left about 3:30 yesterday afternoon in pursuit of the sailboat. They have not returned yet. The wind has been blowing fresh for Twenty-four hours, and it is possible the tug cannot catch the sailboat. Officers along both shores of Lake Michigan have been instructed to watch out for the thieves.

Once they were away from the Sheriff, the sailboat slipped away in the night. The search went on as far as Indiana. They had vanished as quietly as they came. A few months later one was caught.

Arrested a Pirate! Detroit: Barney Williams who was arrested a few days ago has been identified as one of the Mackinac Island pirates by Deputy Sheriff Jaquette. Williams is the man Jaquette captured at the time of the fight with the robbers, but who was captured.

Williams went to prison and never revealed the identities of his partners. To this day, their identities remain a mystery.

Downtown Mackinac Island, see post office at left (circa 1890s)

8   The Pirate Dan Seavey

Perhaps the most famous Great Lakes pirate of all is Dan Seavey, a schooner captain who docked in Escanaba. In the late 1800s and early 1900s, he sailed out into the Great Lakes and plundered wherever and whatever he could.

Born in Bethel, Maine, in 1865, Dan Seavey grew up around sailing and had the love of the sea in his heart. He spent all of his free time around the ships and the men who sailed them. Enchanted with the idea of the sea, he ran away from home at the age of thirteen to sail on tramp steamers. As soon as he was old enough, he joined the Navy. He wasn't one to take orders well, and when his hitch was up, he honorably departed.

Next, Seavey tried working at catching smugglers and trespassers for the Bureau of Indian Affairs on Indian reservations in Wisconsin and Oklahoma. He was proud that he led a group of archaeologists from University of Wisconsin to explore Native American mounds in Marinette County. Still dissatisfied, he moved to Milwaukee where he set himself up in the commercial fishing business and opened a fish market. His love for the sea was reawakened and a love for the Great Lakes was born.

Seavey was a big man. Well over six feet and weighing about 235 pounds, he could be a formidable sight coming at you during a fight. Back then, there were no Marquess of Queensberry Rules, at least not that anyone adhered to.

Seavey married a fourteen-year-old named Mary Plumley, bought a farm, and fathered two daughters, Harriet and Josephine. However, a few years down the road, he caught gold fever through the encouragement of beer magnate Fredrick Pabst and left everything to move to Alaska during the gold rush. He returned from the goldfields empty-handed and broke. He never returned home to his wife and daughter. Mary Seavey didn't see her husband for five years. She searched for him everywhere she could think of. Eventually, a friend told her Dan was working in a saloon in Milwaukee. She confronted Seavey, who was tending bar. No amount of persuading was going to get Dan to come home.

Upon his return in the early 1890s, he settled in Escanaba where he opened a small freight boat service and was married to his second wife. They had a son who died before the age of five. Seavey acquired a schooner named the *Wanderer*, a fifty-foot, two-masted schooner, where he lived part of the time. He also had a room in a boarding house in downtown Escanaba and, in later years, bought a permanent home.

Seavey sailed out of the harbor with a small crew, the first to leave in the spring and the last to arrive in the winter, arriving back as the harbor was closing. His schooner would be coated in ice, the rigging and spars covered with icicles, the deck caked with snow, and the whole ship battered from braving the early winter storms. Most of the local sailors considered Seavey slightly crazy, a notion later confirmed in their eyes.

Using his freight service as a cover, Seavey entered a port after dark with no lights on. Then he and his crew loaded everything on board they could find to steal and set sail before daybreak. He looted anything he could get: cattle, hay, leather goods, and fruit—

Dan Seavey's ship, the *Wanderer*: sometimes it acted as a floating brothel

even women. Everything accessible on the docks that could be loaded before dawn would be gone. Upon the boat's return to Escanaba, he sold it all as legitimate cargo and reaped the profits.

Seavey loved children and spent time talking with them whenever he could. The boys of Escanaba faithfully waited at the docks for his return. He told them stories for hours on end and taught a couple of the boys to sail. One day, an Escanaba boy had been sitting and talking to Seavey for most of the day about sailing and a sailor's life, enthralled with the romance of it. Upon leaving the ship, the boy was grabbed by his father, who spanked him right there on the docks. As he turned to escort his son home, a hand gripped his shoulder and spun him around. The father found himself staring into Dan Seavey's huge chest. Seavey took the father (a prominent businessman) down and resoundingly spanked him, telling him to "leave my shipmates alone."

In Chicago, Seavey unloaded some of his plundered and illegal goods. It was an entry into the black market where no questions were asked. Shipment was always accepted regardless of the type of cargo, and payment was immediately made in cash. Seavey refused to become the agent of any one faction of the underworld, selling to whoever came up with the cash first. This flaunting of independence made him many enemies on both sides of the law.

Seavey had several homes in Escanaba, Frankfort, Milwaukee, and the Garden Peninsula. He also had many hideouts throughout Lake Michigan, and had a homestead on St. Martin's Isle. From there, he ran contraband venison to Chicago in the fall when meat was scarce. The Booth Fish Company, a Chicago-based market with ties to the underworld, wanted Seavey's venison empire. They sent a gang out on one of their boats to take over his territory. After a vicious fight, he was chased away by overwhelming odds. Victorious, the gang started back to Chicago with their news of success. It was just about dusk when Seavey caught up with them in the *Wanderer*. Again, a tough fight ensued, but this time, the pirate had equalized the odds by bringing a cannon that he had pilfered and mounting it on the schooner's bow. The fight ended when Seavey blew the other boat out of the water. None of the gang ever returned to Chicago, and Seavey made it well known that the same fate was in store for anyone else who tried to cross him.

Dan Seavey loved to fight. He carried a pistol with him, and when he was good and drunk, he would occasionally shoot the lights out or put a couple of bullets through the windows. He had a standing challenge that he would always go a few rounds with anyone who thought they could take him. He once sailed to Manistee just to fight a man who had a reputation for having never been beaten. Another incident occurred in Frankfort, where Dan fought a man named Mike Love, in a large circle drawn on the ice in the bay. The fight was much publicized, resulting in a large turnout from the residents. Betting on the outcome seemed to be the spectators' main concern while the two men battled in the snow and cold. It was reported that blows were exchanged for nearly two hours before Dan Seavey finally emerged victorious and announced that drinks would be on him at the nearest saloon.

Another story is from Escanaba, where the *Wanderer* was docked. In the night, Seavey heard heavy footsteps on the deck. Naturally, he went on deck to confront the uninvited guest. The

Dan Seavey and daughter Josephine

mystery man challenged Seavey to come out on the dock, saying, he'd "trim the big piece of meat down to my size." Captain Dan immediately took up the challenge, unaware that the man was a ringer and professional fighter from Chicago. Seavey's enemies were hoping to drive him off. The fighter beat the crap out of Seavey, a rare outcome for Seavey. He refused to accept his defeat. Battered and bleeding, Seavey got to his feet, shaking his fist and yelling at the pro fighter who was walking away, "Come back here tomorrow, you tubercular little shit, and I'll give you another beating."

Charley Hagen, a commercial fisherman from St. Ignace who met Seavey several times, relates a story of Seavey:

> Dan invited us uptown for a drink and none of us really wanted to go because we had business to attend to, but when Dan Seavey wanted you to do something, there wasn't much use to pull back. In Pete Lemmer's saloon, Dan walked up to the bar and yelled for everybody to step up and drink. Two men over in a corner playing cards didn't even turn their heads and Dan pounded on the bar and yelled again for everybody to step up and 'have a drink on Dan Seavey.' When the two men paid no attention, Dan walked over, grabbed them by the backs of their necks and hauled them up to the bar. He handled them like a sack of potatoes. We all drank, but the only man that enjoyed himself much was Dan Seavey.

Seavey would use the *Wanderer* as a floating bordello and casino. He was known to anchor offshore from towns that forbid those kinds of places and let the clientele row out to him. He was known to sail to Sault Ste. Marie with a shipload of prostitutes he would deliver to a brothel there and take others from there back with him, keeping the business fresh with new blood. He was an enterprising individual willing to make money any way he could. Other sailors claimed that Seavey would give you the shirt off his back and then steal it back from you.

On one occasion, a steamboat loaded with shelled corn ran aground on Big Summer Isle in Lake Michigan. Seavey heard about it in Fayette, and while the crew was making it to shore, Seavey sailed off in stormy waters to the wreck. By the time the owners made it out to salvage the wreck, the ship had been stripped clean of cargo, instruments, anchors, ropes, and chains—anything movable was gone!

Seavey salvaged wrecks, some of which he caused, and lured some ships to their doom by putting out false buoys, running them aground. After a wreck, Seavey would wait out of sight on the *Wanderer* until the crew abandoned ship. Then he would transfer their cargo to his ship, sail off, and sell it. This buoy trick had other uses, too.

Seavey once got the crew of the *Nellie Johnson* drunk in Charlevoix (other sources say this happened in Grand Haven), overpowered her captain, tied him up in chains, and tossed him over the side. He then took the schooner to Chicago and sold the ship and the cargo. When he returned to Frankfort, a wealthy man hired him to sail a yacht to Mackinac. Seavey didn't know it at the time, but the man had set him up. As Seavey sailed past Port Betsie, a revenue cutter named the *Tuscarora* slipped out of the darkness and took up pursuit. It had waited out of sight in a cove until Seavey passed it. The chase went on throughout much of the night, but Seavey knew the waters much better than the crew of the cutter. As he passed a harbor buoy, Seavey shot the light out and replaced it with a lantern on a barrel. The *Tuscarora* ran aground, but a change in the wind direction also changed Seavey's luck. The stranded cutter fired a cannon shot across the yacht's bow and he was forced to surrender.

He was taken to Chicago in chains to stand trial for pirating the *Nellie Johnson*. When he appeared before the judge, he cleverly explained that the captain of the schooner got drunk and gave him the ship and cargo in settlement of an old debt. Because the former captain of the *Nellie Johnson* couldn't be found to dispute Seavey's claim, the case fell apart and Dan was released. Ironically, he was then deputized as a U.S. Marshall. The Great Lakes had been nearly impossible to patrol and the law difficult to enforce. It was decided that instead of chasing Seavey, the Government would get him to take the job of patrolling the waters and enforcing the law. The

U.S. Revenue Cutter *Tuscarora*

illegal whiskey smuggling, unlawful fishing, contraband venison, and rampant theft had to be stopped, and Seavey could get into places where regular lawmen couldn't. Also, with Dan now on the side of the law, a good portion of the illegal activities were expected to cease because he was a major contributor to them. Seavey saw it as his chance to start over again, but just because he was now a lawman, his wild ways didn't really change.

Seavey tracked down an outlaw who had been stealing and selling whiskey to the Indians. Dan located him in a saloon in Naubinway. The outlaw told him, "If you can drag me outside, I'll board your schooner for Chicago." After a few drinks, the fight started. Literally, hours of fighting followed, wrecking the saloon. The two occasionally stopped for a drink or two of whiskey. Finally, Seavey slammed the outlaw against the bar, breaking most of the bottles of liquor. Afraid that there wouldn't be enough whiskey left to finish the fight, Seavey knocked the man down and placed a piano on his neck. After downing a few more shots of whiskey, he reconsidered and lifted the piano off the outlaw. Then he asked him to join him in a drink before resuming the fight. The outlaw never got up. He died the following day. Marshall Seavey turned the body

The schooner *R. P. Mason* was pirated by Seavey

over to officials to be buried and turned in his report. He was never asked to answer for the killing.

Because of his reputation, Dan Seavey was unwelcome at Garden, Michgan. He was banned from docking there. This bit of annoyance didn't hinder him much. He would come ashore whenever he wanted, and often, he would anchor in Garden Bay. The locals would disappear as they knew Roaring Dan was trouble. Though Seavey spent quite a bit of time there, the Garden Peninsula never did welcome his presence.

Dan Seavey had other ships besides the *Wanderer*. One was the *R.P. Mason* and another was named the *Harvey Ransom*. Both were fast sailing ships with ample room for cargo. In November of 1913, Seavey found himself aboard the *Harvey Ransom* when the storm of the century hit, the "Big Blow." Considered possibly the worst storm in Great Lakes history, 250 men were lost, nineteen ships were lost and nineteen more were left stranded. This November blizzard helped earn the month its deadly reputation for the worst storms and ship disasters. Captain Dan was sailing the *Harvey Ransom* that night. A witness, Hullie Dalgord, tells the story:

It was either November 7th or 8th, or maybe the 9th or 10th, I'm not sure but I do know it was on a Sunday. The year was 1913 and the storm was the big November blow of that year. The *Ransom*, with Seavey at the helm, was heading for Fayette harbor to pick up a load of baled hay when the northwester struck. Seavey had in his crew two men and a boy. It was a Sunday morning and Seavey saw that he could not make the Fayette harbor so he pulled in behind Burnt Bluff for shelter just a few yards west of the old Robert's fish house. Seavey was a daring man and everything would have been alright if the *Ransom* had not come down on the top of a broken off pond net stake. The stake rammed through her hull and ripped her open so that the water poured in. The *Ransom* was doomed. Seavey and his crew took to a small boat and made the safety of the rocky shore. The sinking schooner drifted ashore. Through the years that followed her bones were broken by waves and ice.

In 1912, Dan Seavey went into another kind of business, the sawmill business. He was known for setting up businesses which he could use as fronts for some of his other illegal operations. He took a liking to a place called Gouley's Bay on the Garden Peninsula near Fairport. Mary Gouley, the bay's only resident, agreed to let Seavey set up a sawmill. She had a farm and a stone quarry.

Seavey worked a deal with local farmers to do their woodcutting while also hauling their grain to market on his ships. Seavey built a house for his second wife, Annie, along with a sawmill and sizable dock for ships to tie up to. An Escanaba newspaper described his place this way, "The Seavey mill was located on a narrow point extending into Gouley's Bay, one corner resting in the water. A dock extending from the mill for a considerable distance into the water for the docking of boats."

This setup seemed to work quite well, and Seavey seemed to be coming into some good money. So much so he decided he needed to raise a ship from the bottom of Fayette harbor. It was the *R. P. Mason*, at one time one of the fastest three-masted schooners to sail the Lakes. He refurbished it and used it for transporting cargo from his sawmill.

In 1915, tragedy struck. Seavey was loading the *R. P. Mason* with a portable sawmill for a job with one of the local farmers. The job lasted all day, and there was a fair amount of drinking involved. Seavey had two helpers, one of whom was a fifteen-year-old boy. At one point, Seavey decided to go take a nap. His two helpers finished the job. Somehow, a can of gasoline was knocked over and a terrific fire broke out. Seavey was sleeping inside the mill. The fifteen-year-old, James Brodie, ran into the flaming mill to get Seavey. He woke him up, but he was already badly burned on his arms and feet. Everything was burning, including the mill and the house. Seavey jumped out a window onto a rocky beach. He was found unconscious several hours later. Brodie didn't make it back out and perished in the fire. The other helper, Lucias Mercier, had a new sailboat tied to the dock. He freed the moorings and tried to get the boat away from the dock. Mysteriously, his boat showed up on the shore the next day, but Mercier was gone. Eventually, his body was recovered on the bottom of the bay. Everything, including the schooner *R. P. Mason*, was burned to cinders.

Seavey was hospitalized while surrounded by insinuations he was guilty of arson and murder. Of course, he wasn't, but his reputation made him an immediate object of suspicion. A coroner's jury in Garden found no evidence of complicity or negligence. Seavey was cleared of any wrongdoing.

Seavey never returned to Gouley's Bay. He recovered in Escanaba and would eventually move to Green Bay. His days on the Lakes were over, and he was in the care of his daughter, Josephine. While Seavey had a long lucrative career, making well over a million dollars in his lifetime in illegal activities, he wasn't as hard-hearted as his occupation made him seem. He gave away all of his money to the poor and to benefit children.

When Seavey died in an old folk's home in Peshtigo, Wisconsin, in 1949, he died quietly, penniless, an end quite unbefitting the wild and rowdy buccaneer who often said he would rather fight than eat.

Seavey goes down in history as the only man formally charged with piracy on the Great Lakes.

Great Lakes piracy ended with Seavey. As time moves forward, the stories of the Great Lakes frontier disappear and are forgotten. There is but little romance in the deeds of the pirates; they lived a life that was hard and brutal at a time when only the strong survived. Piracy no longer exists on the Great Lakes, for which we should all be grateful.

USS Michigan (postcard by L.C. Schauble)

9   Liquor Pirates and the Gray Ghost

Prohibition created a whole new breed of pirate. From 1920 to 1933, the waterways of the Great Lakes became the frontline for smuggling illegal alcohol. From Lake Superior to the East Coast, rum-runners flourished in a chaotic frenzy of obtaining illegal liquor for a suddenly deprived America. People wanted their cocktails. To make matters worse, the Canadian government ruled that it wasn't illegal to sell alcohol to the U.S. setting up a dynamic that would create a criminal element like never before.

From Canada into the U.S., the fastest boats on the water played a game of cat and mouse with the federal authorities; liquor pirates played with both sides. Unfortunately, the government was severely undermanned for such a task. Organized crime thrived, all the while illegally competing for the lucrative alcohol trade. Prohibition made booze worth lots of money, and everyone was trying to cash in. Mobsters, like Al Capone, the Purple Gang, Dutch Shultz and Lucky Luciano, were all fighting for control of the liquor trade. It was worth millions, and many had no problem killing for it. In just one year, $212 million worth of illegal booze crossed the Detroit River alone. That is the equivalent of $2.67 billion today.

From common workers—who simply wanted a drink—to those of high society—who needed to hold their cocktail parties—most people were involved or sympathetic to the smugglers. Judges, law enforcement officers and politicians were all involved in the trade. Many of them allowed properties to be used to store the illegal booze. In one incident, several smugglers were arrested, and about 200 of the locals rose up and freed them from custody.

On the water, mobs would ambush and steal from each other. Liquor was gold, and if one happened to mess with the wrong people, it was also worth a lot of lead. Independent operators and liquor pirates would stop a ship loaded with booze, kill the crew and sell the cargo back to the mobsters. Often reported, it was not unusual for bodies to be floating down the Detroit River after a night of rum-running. It was war along the Canadian border with the U.S. government caught in between in a futile attempt to stop them all. On the Canadian side, docks were lined with every kind of liquor: pick and choose, load up and run for the U.S.

In the winter, cars would cross the ice and load up. Also, many used ice boats, which were swift as the wind: they could cross the river on ice in around 12 minutes. *The Detroit News* described them this way: "A gust of flying snow and perhaps, now and then, a trace of silver canvas stretched taut in the wind and the boats were gone." The police tried putting chains on their cars' tires to chase them; however, even the fastest cars couldn't keep up: "Get near the iceboat and there is a sudden tack, perhaps near enough to send an auto skidding for many feet, and the phantom rum smuggler is hundreds of feet away."

Out of this arose a liquor pirate named the Gray Ghost. His story has been difficult to track down. There were actually three Gray Ghosts operating during Prohibition. One was on the East Coast, near Long Island, NY and another on the West Coast, near Los Angeles, CA. Sorting them out has been difficult. Both *Gray Ghosts* were ships and not individuals.

Though there were liquor pirates galore, for our purposes, the one called the Gray Ghost near Detroit stands out. To this day, his true identity remains a mystery. His ship, also called *Gray Ghost*, was painted gray. He wore a long gray trench coat, a gray hat and a gray mask. Even his pistols and machine gun were painted gray. His ship had a one-pound cannon on its bow. Machine guns mounted on the sides and stern were ready for a fight at any time.

He operated mostly on the Detroit River, avoiding the law by running back and forth between Lake Huron and Lake Erie. He made excursions into Lake Erie to Sandusky and Lake St. Clair. The international border ran through the river, making it a hub for smuggling. Ecorse and Wyandotte were major hotspots for smugglers, and he frequented both places regularly.

The Gray Ghost would look for rum-runners. If stopped on the way to Canada, they were usually carrying a large amount of cash to pay for the liquor, or, if they were U.S. bound, they carried a large cargo of booze worth about $100 a case (or more—a lot of money during the "Roaring 20s") depending on its quality. Either way, it was well worth the risk, and the Ghost would attack their boats. If they put up a fight, they'd be killed; if they didn't, he would let them go. If necessary, he would wipe out a crew and take the cargo. Like the phantom he was named after, he was fast and easily disappeared into the night. Equipped with a 450 horse-power airplane motor, *Gray Ghost* was reputed to be the fastest boat on the water the "fastest boat in the rum-running fleet."

Much of his individual story is obscured by time, but a few incidents have come to the surface, cementing the strange tales that surround the phantomesque qualities of the Gray Ghost and his ship. In February 1929, a Windsor, Ontario newspaper reported:

> The Gray Ghost has materialized again. Listed in Windsor press reports as the victim of a lake tragedy in ice floes off Pelee Island, the phantom flagship of the rum fleet appeared on the streets of Windsor within the last 24 hours. Several residents of the city are witnesses to the fact. What they saw was a long rakish speedboat, grey in color, mounted on two motor lorries (trucks) and being drawn through the city from the La Salle district to some point on the eastern lake front. Identification was established by the words *Gray Ghost* lettered on the bow.
>
> About a week ago, there was a thrilling story printed here that *Gray Ghost* had been sighted in ice floes off Pelee Island with a dead man on board. There was the later story of *Gray Ghost*—with a ghastly crew aboard—floating around Lake Erie with the hand of a dead man guiding the wheel. In Rum Row, it was said that *Gray Ghost* had been lying at dock in La Salle for several weeks and is to be overhauled at an

upriver boathouse in preparation for its spring campaign. Based on a fact that a man named Leo Leonard, who failed to appear in court at Cleveland on a liquor charge, was said to have been found frozen in Lake Erie.

Another story at the same time says:

Now, you see it, now you don't, was an apt description today of the wide search that has been conducted for the rum-running speed boat *Gray Ghost*. At present *Gray Ghost* is not being seen by anyone who will report the vision to authorities, but well-founded reports earlier in the week were that the craft with a dead man at the wheel had been sighted.

Besides himself, the Gray Ghost kept a crew of 3 to 4 manning the ship. It was a deadly, dangerous job. This tale comes from Sandusky, Ohio:

The mystery of *Gray Ghost* -alleged fastest boat of the Lake Erie rum running fleet—was revived today with the finding of a surf-torn body at Orchard Beach by boys playing on the beach. The body may be that of *Gray Ghost's* pilot, Joseph Meyers. *Gray Ghost* put out from Erieau, Ontario on January 9, sailed into the mists of Erie and disappeared.

The Gray Ghost's legend had grown to nearly ridiculous heights. The idea that the missing ship was reported by the newspapers as being piloted by a dead man shows how much his and his ship's reputation had grown into supernatural proportions.

The Purple Gang controlled Detroit's illegal liquor trade. The Gray Ghost would occasionally sell his cargo to the Purple Gang (as well as others) if they were willing to pay the higher price. Liquor was never hard to sell, and Gray Ghost was a daily force to be reckoned with on Lake Erie and the Detroit River.

There isn't an exact date for this, but one night while walking the street, the Gray Ghost was shot and murdered. A car drove by and unloaded a machine gun into him, a typical gangland hit for the day. The reason for the hit was that the Gray Ghost apparently wrote a bad check or two to his liquor suppliers, and they took offense, deciding to get even. Five of them put up $1000 each for an assassin. It was rumored that the assailant was from the Purple Gang, though nothing was ever proven. The Gray Ghost was never identified; he didn't match any records and remains a mystery. His life was fast and violent, as was his death.

Bibliography

Bayfield Historical Society, Bayfield, WI.

Boyd, Richard, Greg Kent, and Janet Defnet. *Archaeology at a Pirate's Den on Lake Michigan.* Unknown publication.

Detroit Free Press. Detroit, Michigan. Various dates.

Escanaba Daily News. Escanaba, Michigan. Various dates.

Giweeonaning, Detour Village 1899-1999, Detour Centennial, 1999.

History of the Upper Peninsula of Michigan. Chicago, IL: Western Historical Company, 1883.

Inland Seas Quarterly Journal, Great Lakes Historical Society, Vermilion, Ohio, 1944 – 1998, various issues.

Johnson, Ida Amanda. *Michigan Fur Trade.* Michigan Historical Commission, 1919.

Lubbock, Basil. *Bully Hayes, South Seas Pirate.* Boston, MA: Charles E. Lauriat Company, 1931.

Niles' National Register. LIV (28 July 1838): 349.

Our Heritage, Garden Peninsula, Delta County, Michigan. Garden Peninsula Historical Society, 1982.

Poppleton, O. *Tales and Traditions of Northern Michigan, Mackinac Island, King Strang and the Mormon, and O'Malley the Irish Dragon.* Historical Collection. Vol. 18, 1891.

Stonehouse, Frederick. *Great Lakes Crime: Murder, Mayhem, Booze & Broads.* Gwinn, MI: Avery Color Studios, 2004.

Stonehouse, Frederick. *Pirates, Crooks & Killers: The Dark Side of the Great Lakes.* Gwinn, MI: Avery Color Studios, 2013.

Van Nord, Roger. *King of Beaver Island: Life and Assassination of James Jesse Strang.* Chicago, IL: University of Illinois Press, 1988.

Williams, Elizabeth Whitney. *A Child of the Sea and Life Among the Mormons.* Brooklyn, NY: J. E. Jewett, 1905.

Websites

William Johnson (navalmarinearchive.com)
https://navalmarinearchive.com/research/docs/william_johnson.html

Bill Johnston: Correcting the Historical Record – Thousand Islands Life Magazine (TILife.org)
https://tilife.org/BackIssues/Archive/tabid/393/articleType/ArticleView/articleId/1032/Bill-Johnston-Correcting-the-Historical-Record.html

USS Michigan – Erie Maritime Museum
https://www.eriemaritimemuseum.org/research-topics/ussmichigan

Erie's Iron Ship, Part 1-The *USS Michigan* Takes on the Timber Pirates - Hagen History Center (eriehistory.org)
https://www.eriehistory.org/blog/eries-iron-ship-part-1-the-uss-michigan-takes-on-the-timber-pirates

Timber Rebellion and the *USS Michigan* – Military History of the Upper Great Lakes (mtu.edu)
https://ss.sites.mtu.edu/mhugl/2017/10/19/timber-rebellion-and-the-uss-michigan/

Michigan's 1st Mail Service and the Great Robbery That Followed.
https://99wfmk.com/mackinac-post-office-robbery-1893

About Mikel B. Classen

Mikel B. Classen has been writing and photographing northern Michigan in newspapers and magazines for forty years, creating feature articles about the life and culture of Michigan's North Country. A journalist, historian, photographer, and author with a fascination of the world around him, he enjoys researching and writing about lost stories from the past. He is founder of the *U.P. Reader* and is a member of the Board of Directors for the Upper Peninsula Publishers and Authors Association. In 2020, Mikel won the Historical Society of Michigan's George Follo Award for Upper Peninsula History.

Classen makes his home in the oldest city in Michigan, historic Sault Sainte Marie. He is also a collector of out-of-print history books, and historical photographs and prints of Upper Michigan. At Northern Michigan University, he studied English, history, journalism, and photography.

His books, *Au Sable Point Lighthouse: Beacon on Lake Superior's Shipwreck Coast* (2014), and *Teddy Roosevelt and the Marquette Libel Trial* (2015) were published by the History Press. His book of fiction, *Lake Superior Tales*, won a 2020 U.P. Notable Book Award. *Points North* (2019), a nonfiction travel book, received the Historical Society of Michigan's, "Outstanding Michigan History Publication," along with a 2021 U.P. Notable Book Award. Since then, he has released, *True Tales: the Forgotten History of Michigan's Upper Peninsula* (2021), and *Faces, Places, & Days Gone By, a Pictorial History of Michigan's Upper Peninsula* (2022). Classen is co-author of the *Yooper Ale Trails* (2023) along with Jon C. Stott all published by Modern History Press. In late 2023, Mikel released his first novel, *The Alexandria Code, an Isabella Carter Adventure*, published by Modern History Press. Mikel's newest endeavor is the Yooper History Hunter Series, the first of which is *Old Victoria, a Copper Country Ghost Town*.

To learn more about Mikel B. Classen and see more of his work, visit www.MikelBClassen.com.

Mikel B. Classen

Index

What Were Pioneer Days *Really* Like in the U.P.?

The combination of mining, maritime, and lumbering history created a culture in the U.P. that is unique to the Midwest. Discover true stories of the rough and dangerous times of the Upper Peninsula frontier that are as enjoyable as they are educational. You'll find no conventional romantic or whitewashed history here. Instead, you will be astonished by the true hardships and facets of trying to settle a frontier sandwiched among the three Great Lakes.

These pages are populated by Native Americans and the European immigrants, looking for their personal promised land—whether to raise families, avoid the law, start a new life or just get rich... no matter what it took. Mineral hunters, outlaws, men of honor creating civilization out of wilderness and the women of strength that accompanied them, the Upper Peninsula called to all. Among the eye-opening stories, you'll find *True Tales* includes:

- Dan Seavey, the infamous pirate based out of Escanaba
- Angelique Mott, who was marooned with her husband on Isle Royale for 9 months with just a handful of provisions and no weapons or tools
- Vigilantes who broke up the notorious sex trafficking rings—protected by stockades, gunmen, and feral dogs—in Seney, Sac Bay, Ewen, Trout Creek, Ontonagon and Bruce Crossing
- Klaus L. Hamringa, the lightkeeper hero who received a commendation of valor for saving the crews of the Monarch and Kiowa shipwrecks
- The strange story of stagecoach robber Reimund (Black Bart) Holzhey

Learn more at www.MikelBClassen.com

From Modern History Press

Featuring more than 150 color photos of the U.P.'s most beautiful, historic, and natural locations

I've spent many years exploring the wilderness of Michigan's Upper Peninsula (U.P.), and one thing has become apparent: no matter what part in which you find yourself, fascinating sights are around every corner. There are parks, wilderness areas and museums. There are ghost towns and places named after legends. There are trails to be walked and waterways to be paddled. In the U.P., life is meant to be lived to the fullest. In this book, I've listed 40 destinations from every corner of the U.P. that have places of interest. Some reflect rich history, while others highlight the natural wonders that abound. So, join in the adventures. The Upper Peninsula is an open book--the one that's in your hand.

"Without a doubt, Mikel Classen's *Points North* needs to be in every library, gift shop and quality bookstore throughout state. Not only does Classen bring alive the U.P. through his polished words, his masterful use of color photography also makes this book absolutely beautiful. *Points North* will long stand as a tremendous tribute to one of the most remarkable parts of our country."
—Michael Carrier, author, *Murder on Sugar Island*

"Mikel Classen's love for Michigan's Upper Peninsula shines from every page in *Points North*, a fascinating insider's guidebook to the exceptional beauty and history of Michigan's far north. Whether you're still in the planning stages of your trip, or you're looking back fondly on the memories you created—even if you wish merely to enjoy a virtual tour of the Upper Peninsula's natural wonders from the comfort of your armchair, you need this book."
—Karen Dionne, author, *The Marsh King's Daughter*

Learn more at **www.PointsNorthBooks.com**

From Modern History Press

Enjoy a Visual Trip to See How People Lived and Worked in the U.P. in Centuries Past!

Classen's pictorial history is the next best thing to a time machine, as we get a front-row seat in the worlds of shipping and shipwrecks, iron and copper mining, timber cutting, hunting and fishing and the everyday lives of ordinary folks of Michigan's Upper Peninsula across more than 100 years. Faces, Places, and Days Gone By peers into our past through the lenses of those that lived and explored it. See what they saw as time passed and how the U.P. evolved into the wonderous place we know today.

From the author's unique collection, witness newly restored images from long lost stereoviews, cabinet cards, postcards and lithograph engravings. Join us on a visual journey to relive some of those moments, and discover a unique heritage through those faces and places. From the Soo to Ironwood, from Copper Harbor to Mackinaw Island--you'll never see the U.P. in quite the same way!

"Historian Mikel B. Classen has achieved a work of monumental importance. Drawing from his collection of archival photographs, Classen takes readers on a journey in time that gives rare insight into a vanished world."

—Sue Harrison, international bestselling author of *The Midwife's Touch*

"This book provides a fascinating and nostalgic look at more than a century of Upper Michigan photography. From images of iron mines and logging to Sunday drives and palatial hotels, you are bound to be in awe of this chance to visit the past."

—Tyler R. Tichelaar, award-winning author of *Kawbawgam: The Chief, The Legend, The Man*

Learn more at www.MikelBClassen.com

3

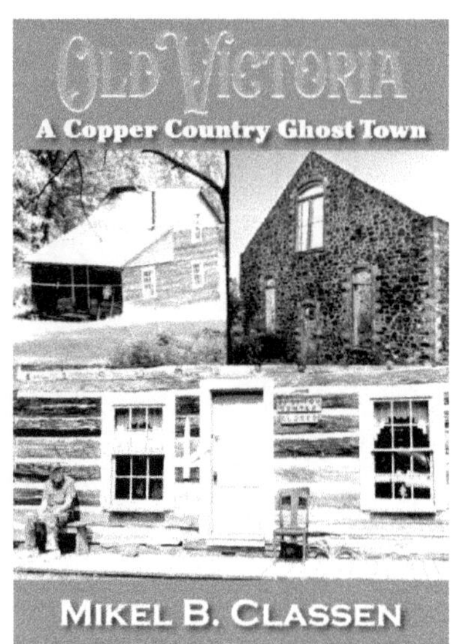

Old Victoria, a ghost town from the copper boom, shows what life was like homesteading in Michigan's Upper Peninsula. Over the years, some of the site has been destroyed or has collapsed; still, many of Old Victoria's original homesteads remain standing. Thanks to the efforts of a local group, The Society for the Restoration of Old Victoria, quite a few of the buildings have been restored and refurnished in their original condition. Unlike Fayette, the U.P.'s best-known ghost town and a small shipping port on Lake Michigan, Victoria is a remote, rugged mining town, buried in the Ontonagon wilderness.

Join Mikel B. Classen, the Yooper History Hunter, on a romp through time with two dozen photographs that portray more than a century of Old Victoria!

"Both history and travel guide, this thoroughly researched and gracefully written book—illustrated with both historical and contemporary photographs—is a must-read for people planning visits to lesser-known parts of the western Upper Peninsula."
—Jon C. Stott, author *Paul Bunyan in Michigan*

"*Old Victoria: A Copper Country Ghost Town*, the inaugural volume of the Yooper History Hunter Series, offers a colorful, up-close look at the life of a small mining town in one of the remotest corners of Michigan. Painstakingly researched, but an effortless read."
—Victor R. Volkman, *Marquette Monthly*

Learn more at www.MikelBClassen.com

From Modern History Press